Lake Effect

Lake Effect

ALONG

SUPERIOR'S

SHORES

Erika Alin

University of Minnesota Press Minneapolis / London

The frontispiece photograph was taken by the author at Artist's Point in Grand Marais, Minnesota, October 1998.

Map of Lake Superior was created by Parrot Graphics.

Published by the University of Minnesota Press
111 Third Avenue South, Suite 290
Minneapolis, MN 55401-2520
http://www.upress.umn.edu

Library of Congress Cataloging-in-Publication Data

Alin, Erika G.
 Lake effect : along Superior's shores / Erika Alin.
   p.   cm.
 Includes bibliographical references.
 ISBN 0-8166-4114-5 (PB : alk. paper)
 1. Superior, Lake, Region—Description and travel.   2. Superior, Lake, Region—History, Local.   3. Superior, Lake, Region—History.   4. Natural history—Superior, Lake, Region.   5. Landscape—Superior, Lake, Region.   I. Title.
 F552 .A44 2003
 917.74'90444—dc21

2002154133

Printed in the United States of America on acid-free paper

The University of Minnesota is an equal-opportunity educator and employer.

12 11 10 09 08 07 06 05 04 03   10 9 8 7 6 5 4 3 2 1

Contents

Preface

AFTER MORE THAN A DECADE IN THE MIDWEST, I AM still uncomfortable being landlocked. Growing up, dividing my time between northern Long Island and western Sweden, I took the ocean as much for granted as the air I breathed. I moved to Minnesota by chance, to pursue an unexpected job offer, and had it not been for Lake Superior's waters, I am convinced that I would have headed back east years ago. Lake Superior saved me from geographic claustrophobia, offering what nothing else in the landscape could: an immediate sense of connection, a shorthand for converting the strange into the familiar and imbuing my surroundings with the affinity to and awareness of a place where I feel at home. After countless trips north from my Saint Paul home, its waters still draw me like a lightning rod.

These essays are the product of my journey into the natural and human landscape of the lake. They sample the rich diversity in geologic history, natural habitat, and cultural experience that has shaped Lake Superior's shores. Various regions of the lake offer the visitor different experiences, depending on the composition of the bedrock, the force of wind and weather, and the long line of human inhabitants who have crossed the shores. Ontario's granite outcrops leave a different impression than Michigan's sandstone shelves. Mining, a critical cause of early European settlement, left its mark mainly inland of the Minnesota and Michigan coasts. Logging extended its reach more uniformly, but although protected patches of old-growth forest remain in several places, those hoping for a wilderness experience may be better off in Ontario. The different statements that varied regions make are heightened by the fact that several species of trees, plants, and animals reach the limits of their natural range in the Superior area. Apart from isolated locations, yellow birches are uncommon on the north shore, sugar maples and eastern hemlocks grow most abundantly on glacial deposits and loamy soils farther south, and the endangered piping plover nests mainly on Michigan beaches.

Diversity is apparent not only between but also within regions and often even at specific destinations. Many of the places visited in this book provide a menu of natural environments to choose from: rocky ledges or outcrops, small sheltered beaches, pine-clad northern ridges, southern hardwood slopes, inland streams, and more. I let my interests guide me in choosing which of a nearly infinite array of possible areas to visit, and which components of each place's natural and human history to explore. I am confident that others would make different choices, each adding a perspective, whether in word, image, or even a thought or experience shared with no one else, to the chronology of human encounters with the lake. Yet for all the variations, as anyone who travels around the lake is likely to notice, the Superior landscape is also full of reassuring similarities. The north woods ties its ribbon around the length of the shore, and fortunately, more than a few bits and pieces of knowledge about flora, fauna, and even human history acquired in one area can be transferred to another.

This book begins with a visit to the lower Saint Louis River, which, having its outlet through Duluth-Superior harbor, forms the southern extension of Lake Superior's Minnesota shore. Proceeding roughly clockwise around the lake, I follow the Minnesota and Ontario coastlines, taking in Kitchi Gammi Park, the Temperance River, Crosby Manitou State Park, Grand Marais, the Boundary Waters Canoe Area Wilderness, the Coldwell Peninsula, and Lake Superior Provincial Park. Moving west along the Michigan and Wisconsin coasts, I explore the natural and human histories of the Keweenaw Peninsula, the Porcupine Mountains, and Chequamegon Bay before ending at the Brule River, east of Duluth-Superior, in northwestern Wisconsin. The order of the essays suggests a predetermined circular route around the lake, but like many good journeys this one has been full of detours. It began with a focus on natural and geologic history, but the discovery of new places frequently provided a context for delving into other areas. The essays accordingly explore topics as diverse as the names of rivers, early Native American settlement, French explorers and missionaries, geologic history, women botanists, ring-billed gulls, and the Group of Seven artists. Quite often, the essays probe particular phenomena and connections that have intrigued me but are not necessarily defining characteristics of the places.

Much more could have been said about the rapid pace of development, including the growing tourist economy, that is jeopardizing the natural environment of the Lake Superior region. May the day never come when large swaths of the shore will be devoid of genuine natural places, when for every vista there will be another highway pullout, and for every bend in the trail another bench or marker. But I also use those pullouts, stop at the gas stations and cafés, and in winter abandon campgrounds for highway motels. In the end, all that each of us can do is to try, wherever we may be, to find natural places that connect with our lives, that metaphorically weave together our experiences and understandings.

Many people have helped me in this pursuit over the years. Park rangers on both sides of the border have shared information and tips on places to visit. Staff and librarians at state and county historical societies and departments of natural resources have assisted me in locating documents, reports, and other primary source materials. Tim Cochrane, Cynthia Cone, Ted Hodapp, Patricia Maus, Richard Ojakangas, and Carol Urness have generously read and commented on earlier versions of several of the essays. And Michael, my friend and partner on life's journeys, has crossed many a milepost with me, encouraging me forward with his unshakable faith in my endeavors.

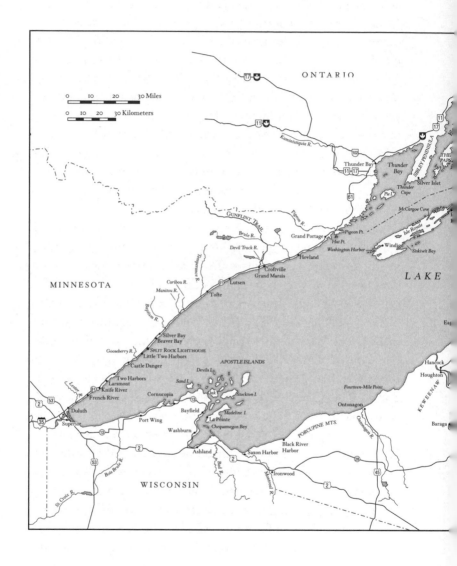

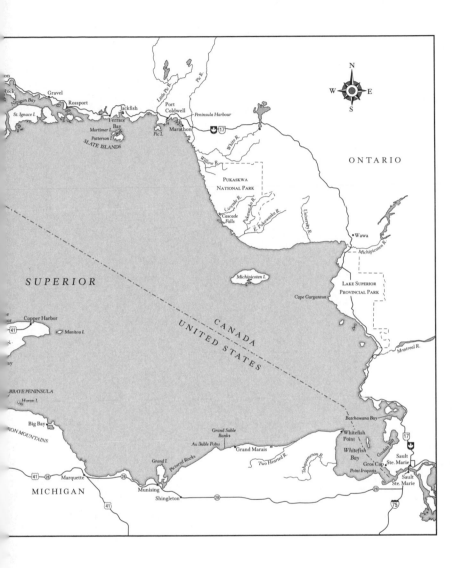

Wild River

EVEN FROM THE SAFETY OF THE SWINGING BRIDGE, the force of the Saint Louis River is downright unnerving. In springtime the river could easily be the miniature Snake or Columbia of the midwestern frontier, and as it courses through the rock-lined lower gorge, human life seems not only vulnerable but insignificant before its brute and indiscriminate force. Looking down, I cannot help but feel a quivering of the ancient peril on which the survival of early man depended. Yet, like its western counterparts, the Saint Louis River no longer freely seeks its own course. Half a mile upstream of the Swinging Bridge, the Thomson dam, one of five dams on the lower river, impounds the largest hydroelectric reservoir in Minnesota and controls the amount of water entering the lower gorge. A bit farther downstream, the Fond du Lac dam regulates the remainder of the river's descent toward Lake Superior. Fortunately, neither dam is visible from the bridge, and looking down at the raging current, it is still possible to imagine the Saint Louis as it once was—wild and untamed.

Flowing 179 miles from its source in Seven Beaver Lake on the border of Minnesota's Iron Range, the Saint Louis is Lake Superior's largest American tributary. It enters the lake through an island-studded estuary some 15 miles east of Jay Cooke State Park, where the Swinging Bridge is located. The estuary was once the river's mouth, but as the lake's northeastern shore rebounded from the glaciers' weight, more water moved toward the southwestern end of the basin, gradually flooding the lower Saint Louis. Today, the largely undeveloped upper estuary provides critical habitat for over 250 species of migratory birds. As have the river and the whitefish and sturgeon that once spawned in large numbers above Fond du Lac, the estuary habitat has been threatened by nonpoint pollution, upstream dam construction, leaky landfills, and industrial effluent, as well as the overall decline in water quality resulting from the development of Duluth-Superior as a major international port.

The Saint Louis approaches the harbor from the southwest, after making a large inland loop from its headwaters in the northeastern Minnesota highlands. Its watershed is huge compared with those of rivers farther up the north shore, and its final descent toward the lake is fairly steady. While rocky and rapid-filled, the lower river has no high fall. Like its northern relations, the river has the telltale tea color that comes from having traveled over boggy terrain, and as the mid-April sun beats down on its waters, the damp, earthy smell of springtime fills the air. One by one, thick chunks of ice pass under the bridge. I fasten my eyes on a chunk and quickly turn around, the suspension rails moaning as I shift my weight across the planks. Yet the ice has outpaced me, and I can barely make out its bobbing form a short distance downstream.

True to its name, the bridge can easily be made to swing. As two boys jump up and down on the planks, the sounds of squeaking rails and shouting children rise over the rushing waters. The bridge is firmly anchored to large cement pillars at each end, and the noise it makes usually far exceeds any actual swinging motion.

But apparently it was not always this safe. A park sign describes how the original log supports were replaced by stone pillars, reinforced with concrete, in the mid-1930s. A few years later, the bridge was raised by several feet, yet this did not prevent it from being carried downstream by spring meltwaters in 1950 and having to be rebuilt. Looking down at the swollen current, I can imagine such an event repeating itself in my lifetime.

When I come to Jay Cooke, I always make the same round, following a trail on the river's southern bank downstream from the Swinging Bridge. The trail is muddy, and where it narrows to descend downhill toward the river, I grasp a trunk for safety and step across some lingering ice and onto the leafy duff. One winter is all it takes for the crisp, colorful carpets of fall to turn soggy and ashen. Before long, however, the leaves of maple, aspen, birch, and basswood will begin to add fullness to the canopy, and on the ground, fern, horsetail, wild ginger, alder, willow, and blueberry shrubs will come into leaf. For now, the sun still streams through the bare branches, and there is not even a tentative sign of the blue violets, bunchberries, wood anemones, and lilies-of-the-valley that will soon grace the side of the trail.

Dark, jagged rock beds rise ominously at steep angles out of the river, the white currents rearing like stallions against their peaks. The beds of the lower Saint Louis are, in my view, the most unusual and dramatic-looking rock formations in the north shore area. They span nearly twice the geologic history of the hardened lava flows that appear farther up the Minnesota shore. They had their origins in the eroded muds and sands that washed off the land and came to rest on the floor of a warm, shallow sea almost two billion years ago. The sediments originally settled close to the shore, forming vast underwater deltas of sorts, yet as they accumulated, they became unstable and began to slide downslope toward the deeper sea floor. As they did so, they created and became caught up in powerful sediment-laden currents. Where the gradient leveled off, the currents released sands and heavier grains onto the sea floor. The finer, darker muds, which remained suspended longer, settled out on top of them. Over time, the sediment layers piled up thousands of feet thick on the bottom of the sea.

Later yet, they were further transformed, under the heat, pressure, and shifting of a major regional mountain-building episode, into beds of dark, mud-derived slate and coarser, sandier, and lighter-colored graywacke. The beds remained buried until during the past one and a half million years, when several waves of glaciation descended over North America. The glaciers removed softer, overlying rocks and worked and reworked the beds, leaving small boulder-formed potholes, striations, and other indicators of their passage.

Some twelve thousand years ago, toward the end of the Wisconsin glaciation, formidable torrents of meltwater began to flow through the Saint Louis. The river became the largest tributary of Glacial Lake Duluth, a precursor to Lake Superior, whose surface reached nearly five hundred feet above the present shoreline. Bereft of vegetation, the postglacial landscape eroded easily, and much of the land in Jay Cooke today consists of silts, clays, and sands that were deposited atop the tilted older slates in a vast underwater delta where the river emptied into the lake. Had I been standing on the Swinging Bridge back then, I would have been covered by hundreds of feet of soggy sediments. As the meltwaters receded and Lake Duluth's surface dropped, the Saint Louis was forced to cut its way through the dry hills of the delta, eventually exposing the tilted slate and graywacke beds along a section of its channel.

The beds in Jay Cooke make for some interesting contrasts. The slates are a fine dark gray and have slightly pocketed surfaces and uneven edges. A few display hardened ripple marks from the ancient sea floor. Slate is a hard and brittle rock, fracturing easily along the planes in which it formed, and slender, angular, dark shingles rest in droves in sheltered areas on the riverbank. As for the graywackes, the most appealing beds are smooth-surfaced and unusually light in color. Gently furrowed and wide-bottomed, they rise from the river's channel like giant elephant backs about a quarter of a mile upstream of the Swinging Bridge.

Perhaps more than any other river, the Saint Louis is a place to ponder the rich, complicated history of early European trade and settlement along the Superior shore. Although the Jesuit missionary Claude Jean Allouez had paddled the western Superior shore in 1667, the first European known to have actually ventured up the Saint Louis River was the Frenchman Daniel Greysolon, sieur Du Luth, who visited the Superior region in 1679–80. The French took to referring to the southwestern area of the lake as Fond du Lac, the "farther end or head of the lake." While the Saint Louis was probably eventually named in honor of the French king, the river appears on early French maps as the Rivière du Fond du Lac. The French made only sporadic use of the river, and it was during the latter decades of the 1700s, after Britain had taken over France's North American territories, that the Saint Louis became an important trade route, providing access not only to the Minnesota-Ontario border lakes region but also, by way of the Savanna portage and Sandy Lake, to the upper Mississippi watershed. By then, with the beaver all but extinct in the East, the region had become prized as a source of thick, high-quality pelts, found where winters are long and food supplies ample. Traders who plied the Saint Louis and Lake Superior's shores continued to use the name Fond du Lac, or Head of the Lakes.

Most of the merchants who entered the western fur trade under the British were young Englishmen, often Scots employed by the Montreal-based North West Fur Company, an alliance of previously competing small trade groups, which built an outpost on the Wisconsin side of the river's mouth in 1793. Relative to their French counterparts, the new merchants had little knowledge of native languages and customs and a more contemptuous attitude toward Indian life. Since the area's native communities had, in any event, been allies of France, the new merchants entered into partnerships with French trade operators who remained on the lake and had family and other connections with local trappers and suppliers. Moreover, the North West Fur Company continued to use the legendary French-speaking voyageurs to paddle and portage their canoe loads of pelts and trade goods.

The decision of the United States in 1816 to ban English and other foreign traders from its territory and assert its authority over the Head of the Lakes area, likewise, meant little more than another change in employer for the voyageurs, whose ranks were by then filled mainly with French-Indian métis. John Jacob Astor's American Fur Company, which built its first trade post in the area at the present-day village of Fond du Lac on the Saint Louis River, relied largely on the métis and on Indian-speaking French Canadian traders and apparently considered one voyageur capable of doing the work of four Americans.

An arduous seven-mile portage, which began shortly upriver from Fond du Lac, skirted the unnavigable waters of the Saint Louis River's lower gorge. I try to imagine the sighs of countless voyageurs as they hauled the cargo-laden canoes over the steep, clayey terrain of the so-called Grand Portage. Lieutenant James Allen, who led the military escort and maintained the journal for Henry Schoolcraft's 1832 expedition in search of the source of the Mississippi, described the portage, which took three to five days to complete in good weather, as "a little, narrow, crooked path . . . winding round trees, thru marshes, over ridges, and across ravines." "No idea can be found of the difficulty of this portage without witnessing it," he wrote. In the end, I do not envy the voyageurs their back-breaking work on the portage. But I do envy what they saw, the Saint Louis River in its natural state.

The portage took its name from the longer detour around the falls of the lower Pigeon River to the north, the real so-called Grand Portage. Both routes were used to reach the beaver-rich Lake of the Woods region and were surveyed in the 1820s as part of ongoing efforts to resolve uncertainties over the location of the international border west of Lake Superior. The 1842 Webster-Ashburn Treaty settled on the Pigeon River route. Had the border instead extended northwestward from the mouth of the Saint Louis, England and, later, Canada would have acquired Lake Superior's Minnesota shore and Iron Range.

By the time the American Fur Company arrived on the scene, the days of the fur trade were numbered. By the early 1830s, the company had diversified into commercial fishing, and two decades later, with the Great Lakes beaver, marten, and otter all but extinct and the fur hat fallen from fashion, the trade collapsed entirely. For the Ojibwe and the métis, who fished for trout and whitefish and harvested wild rice and maple syrup in the Saint Louis region and had become increasingly integrated into the trade-based economy at Fond du Lac, the decline of the fur trade brought hardship. The Fond du Lac band, according to Allen, was "miserably poor" and heavily dependent on the trade post. In 1854, the Treaty of La Pointe opened the Minnesota shore to white settlement, bringing further loss to the area's Ojibwe. In exchange for government liquidation of its trade debts and the receipt of an annual annuity as well as a few goods and services, the community ceded its lands and resettled on the Fond du Lac Indian Reservation, which was created under the treaty.

For nearly two centuries, fur traders had moved progressively westward to keep up with the beaver's diminishing range. Along with the beaver, the white pine forests of the eastern United States were being overharvested and depleted. Loggers too had been moving westward along the Great Lakes watershed, using the same rivers that had carried the voyageurs' pelt-laden canoes to move their timber out of the forest. By the early 1860s, they had reached the white pine stands around the Saint Louis River. Tall and strong, the white pine was the most sought-after early timber, and while they lasted, Lake Superior's stands provided wood for fuel, houses, barns, factories, railroad ties, and bridges on the ever expanding western frontier. The large watershed of the Saint Louis afforded plenty of log-driving streams. Early logging operations used horse sleds to skid felled timber on ice tracks to the stream banks in winter. The livelihoods of early lumberjacks and millers depended on a good spring thaw, when the meltwaters ran high enough to float the logs to sawmills in the small town of Thomson, just outside the western border of Jay Cooke State Park, or, in some cases, to Fond du Lac, from where they could be rafted down to Duluth. The park headquarters today sit on former pasturelands owned by the Thomson sawmill.

With the coming of the railroad, spring log drives became a thing of the past. In 1870, the Lake Superior and Mississippi Railroad was completed between Saint Paul and Duluth, running through Thomson and following the northern bank of the Saint Louis River east to Fond du Lac and Duluth. The scenic Thomson–Fond du Lac stretch of the track used steep downgrades and high wooden trestles to cross the clayey riverside terrain, and ever a challenge to maintain, it was discontinued in favor of a more direct route to Duluth in 1888. The former railroad right-of-way is today a bike path just outside the park's borders.

Plans for laying rails were on an ambitious scale, and the same year that the Lake Superior and Mississippi line was completed, the first tracks were put down for the Northern Pacific Railroad, across the river from Thomson. Both railroads were financed largely by the Philadelphia-based banker Jay Cooke, who had sent his agent, Rice Harper, to explore the potential of the Saint Louis area in 1866. Cooke himself visited the sleepy town of Duluth two years later and quickly saw the potential to use the Great Lakes to connect East Coast cities with the western frontier. Timber, grain, and cattle could be moved by rail and loaded onto eastbound ships at Duluth. Manufactured goods could go the other way. East would meet West at Northern Pacific Junction, between the towns of Thomson and Carlton, on the Saint Louis River's southern bank, where a wooden sign reads, "On February 15, 1870, the construction of the Northern Pacific railroad was commenced." As an aside, the name of Thomson is thought to be associated either with David Thompson, minus the *p,* the English explorer and North West Company surveyor who led a border survey of the Saint Louis–Lake of the Woods route, or J. Edgar Thomson, a powerful industrialist and a friend of Jay Cooke, who invested in a number of the latter's local ventures and served as director of the Northern Pacific.

Attracted to large-scale projects, Cooke invested heavily in developing the Head of the Lakes region. His company bought up vast timber stands and farmlands and financed much of Duluth's infrastructure and early economic expansion. Though named after the first white man known to have paddled the Saint Louis River, Duluth was sometimes referred to as "Jay Cooke's town" and grew quickly, attracting both capital and settlers. Cooke, however, had agreed to market a million dollars in bonds for the construction of the Northern Pacific. A decade earlier, he had almost single-handedly financed the Civil War for the North with a hugely successful sale of "five-twenty" government bonds through extensive newspaper advertisements and editorials. The Northern Pacific, however, turned out to be a much tougher sell. Unfamiliar with the country's northwestern hinterland, many people feared investing in the railroad, and by 1873, Jay Cooke & Co. was overextended, with tracks having been laid no farther west than Bismarck. The company's subsequent failure set off a financial crisis that reverberated across the country and triggered a massive flight of investors and settlers from Duluth.

By the century's end, however, Cooke's vision for the Head of the Lakes began to pay off. As the Northern Pacific extended westward, timber and grain began arriving by rail to be processed in local saw and flour mills before being shipped east, along with ore and other products. Duluth became a rapidly expanding port city, and in the 1880s, the hills around the Saint Louis were quarried extensively for Fond du Lac sandstone, which was used in the construction of brownstone schools, churches, warehouses, and Romanesque revival mansions. Yet economic development depended not only on connecting the city with domestic and international markets but also on ensuring a sufficient source of power with which to fuel its mills. In 1885, Cooke, having recovered his fortune through mineral investments out West, bought land to build a hydroelectric dam just west of Thomson on the Saint Louis. The Thomson dam was completed in 1907, two years after Cooke's death. In 1915, the Saint Louis River Water Power Company deeded about 2,300 acres of land that, along with later additions, today make up Jay Cooke State Park. The river's wild waters, however, no longer flowed freely in the lower gorge.

Half a mile or so downstream of the Swinging Bridge, a slender, tree-clad island parallels the river's southern bank. I frequently use the island as a yardstick against which to measure seasonal variations in the river's flow. When the river is low in late summer, a placid current, easily crossed by way of a few rocks, separates the beds that rim the island from those that line the shore. Dry pebbles lie undisturbed in previously submerged potholes in the beds, and slightly above the water's reach, a few ashen patches of silt and sediment are all that remain of the bright, tidy bands that once the early summer meltwaters had receded, briefly ran as white as chalk against the dark rock. Once atop the island, the soils are hard and dry, and the trees are firmly anchored and in full leaf.

Looking out at the river in springtime, however, I find it hard to believe that I will ever walk in the island's small forest again. The forceful current has all but engulfed the trees, and naked branches flay like arms in search of rescue in the water. The nearest land in sight is straight across the river, on the opposite bank. Yet, judging from the size of its trunks, the forest has already survived a good many floods. The currents will do their damage, injuring or uprooting vulnerable trees and leaving one or two piles of driftwood teetering atop the island's beds. But if previous years are any indication, most of the island's trees will not meet their destiny this spring.

Much as I like to walk in the small forest, I prefer the river in springtime, when the solid earth of the island gives way to the raging waters. The currents evoke an instinctual sense of foreboding, a primitive trepidation that leaves me checking and rechecking my step as I make my way downstream along the water's edge. Fortunately, it will take more than a dam to rob the Saint Louis River of its springtime fury, and until the meltwaters recede, I will continue to imagine the river as it once used to be. Wild and untamed.

The Gulls of Kitchi Gammi

IT IS MID-APRIL AND RING-BILLED GULLS HAVE
recently arrived on the shores of Kitchi Gammi Park. Chances
are good that they will remain in the area until fall, nesting in and
around the Duluth-Superior harbor and feeding on food scraps
people leave behind. Mine is the only car in the parking lot, and
I have been watching a dozen or so gulls with my binoculars
through the windshield. In the way of picnics, foghorns, and lake
breezes, gulls have a quaint association with summertime. Yet the
ring-billed is one of the most common gulls in the country, a dan-
delion of the bird world that frequents not only lake and ocean
coasts but also city parks and parking lots. John James Audubon
called it simply the "common American gull," and in many places
today it is considered a nuisance. Few binoculars, I suspect, will
point in its direction on Kitchi Gammi's shores this summer.

This underappreciation is a shame, for ring-bills are beautiful
birds. Hunkered down on the rocks against the wind, they look
calm, inquisitive, and innocently beseeching. Resting on the water,
they are buoyant and composed, even in rough weather. Like the

11

larger herring gull, which also nests on the Superior shore, adult ring-bills have snow-white heads, chests, and underbodies, light gray mantles, and black, white-banded wing tips. Yet with soft, shade-sculpted heads, compact bodies, and dainty beaks, they display little of the herring's menacing demeanor. Small, distinctive features, moreover, endow ring-bills with a greater symmetry. Whereas the herring gull has a yellow bill, flesh-colored legs, and no beak ring, the ring-bill's beak and legs are both yellow, and its beak ring and wing tips equally black. Even more stunning, the pale yellow eye of a breeding bird is encircled by an orange red orbital ring, the bright color of which is reproduced in the gape. The herring may be the most widespread gull in North America, but the ring-bill is, I think, by far the more attractive of the two.

In the air, a ring-bill's movements are as impressive as its looks. When searching for food, it can be seen hanging lyrically over the water's surface, suspended as if by an invisible line just inches above the waves. Hovering nearly motionless against the wind, its wings are extended like large sails, and it is the epitome of aerodynamic grace, living up to its reputation as the acrobat of the gull world.

Yet appearances tell only half the story, for like the much maligned crow, the ring-bill is an intelligent bird, ever alert and quick to respond to danger. It is also highly sociable, endowed with a well-developed sense of community, and prefers to nest in large colonies, which often number in the thousands. The birds within a colony, especially the males, can be quarrelsome, but unlike the noisier herring gull, ring-bills tend to be fairly quiet and subdued except when alarmed or feeding. During the morning I spend at Kitchi Gammi, there are many long spells of calm and silence in the flock.

Ring-bills usually mate for life. The two birds find each other anew on the breeding grounds every spring after a winter spent apart. The birds in one of the pairs that I have been watching on the shore have stood side by side, each a near mirror image of the other, for half an hour, occasionally rubbing necks, touching beaks, and cooing softly. Both mates are diligent parents and work together to gather weeds and grasses to build their nest and incubate their eggs, and to feed and raise their young. In a normal brood of three chicks, it is not uncommon for two to survive to fledge, which takes a little over a month. Devoted to their mates, their offspring, and their community, ring-bills, it seems to me, embody many qualities that we humans admire.

Even if one were not inclined to credit them with lofty looks or admirable traits, ring-bills perform a beautifying function on the shore, nourishing large colonies of orange lichen with their nutrient-rich droppings. The name for this lichen, *Xanthoria elegans,* elegant or jewel lichen, is an apt description of the brilliant color and intriguing pattern the colonies lend to the dark basalt. Jewel lichen are common on ocean-fronting cliffs, especially on limestone, around the world, and as their presence on the Superior shore suggests, they also grow well on other rocks whose surfaces have been enriched by bird droppings. They can often be relied on as indicators of perch rocks and nesting cliffs. The distribution of white droppings makes it easy to see which rocks the gulls prefer at Kitchi Gammi, yet because the low-lying shore is easily wave-washed, there are few lichen. The ledges at Gooseberry Falls and Artist's Point in Grand Marais are much better bets for seeing *Xanthoria elegans.*

For much of the twentieth century, it would have been unusual to find colonies of ring-bills on Lake Superior's northern shore. In the middle and late 1800s, they and other gulls suffered a drastic population decline as a result of human encroachment on their nesting habitat and the popularity of their white feathers on women's hats and gowns. In 1916, however, they received protected status under the U.S.–Canada Migratory Bird Treaty and, after a sluggish start, began to stage a remarkable recovery throughout their former range.

Like many other gulls, ring-bills are opportunistic feeders. The gull's voracious appetite seems to have been recognized as early as the ancient Greeks, from whom the Latin genus name *larus,* meaning a ravenous seabird, was derived. While ring-bills are less fond than herring gulls of landfills, such as the one on nearby Wisconsin Point, they will generally make do with anything from small rodents, worms, insects, fish, and crustaceans to human refuse. They are also versatile nesters, breeding anywhere from on their preferred lakeshore, marsh, and island sites to city parks and concrete piers. Ring-bills, it is hard not to conclude, have adapted well to civilization. Moreover, in staging their impressive recovery and in overtaking and even edging out herring gulls in some areas, they have had the added advantage of a relatively long life span, often living to ten years or more, and a high rate of reproductive success. These same characteristics and their earlier arrival on their nesting grounds have enabled them to threaten the breeding habitat and, through predation, the chick survival rates of the piping plover and common tern, which also nest in the Duluth-Superior harbor area.

Despite their recovery, until the mid-1970s, ring-billed gulls nested mainly on the lower Great Lakes and were rarely seen in the Superior region. Scattered reports of ring-bills began to surface in the 1960s, yet no nesting colony was known to exist in the Duluth-Superior area until 1974, when some five hundred pairs were found breeding on the property of Minnesota Power's Hibbard Power Plant on the lower Saint Louis River. By 1979, three thousand ring-bills and a handful of herring gulls were nesting in and around the Duluth-Superior harbor. Present estimates of the summer population range in the tens of thousands, and record nesting populations of both ring-bills and herrings have been present in the area during the past decade.

It has been speculated that changing water levels and growing recreational activity on the lower Great Lakes have disrupted traditional nesting sites, while increased development on the upper lakes has brought a corresponding rise in human-generated food sources. Lake levels were especially low in the late 1970s and early 1980s, when ring-bills first began nesting in the Duluth-Superior harbor in large numbers. Researchers have also pointed to an abundant supply of alewives, which form a staple fish for the ring-bill, as a possible explanation for the increase in overall population numbers. Ring-bill numbers have increased much more dramatically than those of herring gulls on the Minnesota shore, possibly because the latter also make use of rocky islets in the Superior National Forest and extend their breeding range farther north in Canada and Alaska, thus having greater nesting options. Yet despite dramatic surges in their numbers in the Duluth-Superior harbor, ring-bills still breed more abundantly on the lower Great Lakes than on the upper, as well as on the Saint Lawrence River and around pothole lakes in the northern American and Canadian prairies.

At a glance, especially when seen from a distance, ring-bill and herring gulls can be quite difficult to tell apart. Herrings tend to nest in smaller colonies or even single pairs, and making use of rocky islets, they also breed not only farther inland but also farther north, in Cook and Lake Counties, along the Minnesota shore. Yet there are many places, including parks, harbors, and parking lots, where the species mingle. Fortunately, in many of these places, it is easy to get close enough to see whether the birds have the telltale black ring around their beaks. Especially around Duluth-Superior, ring-bills can usually be assumed to far outnumber herrings, except at landfills and garbage dumps. The problem of identification, however, is trickier when it comes to immature birds. Ring-bills and herrings take three and four years, respectively, to assume adult plumage, and until then the young of both species have black-tipped bills, flesh-colored legs, and a mottled brown appearance. Surrounded by herring look-alikes, immature ring-bills are best identified by their lighter shade of brown.

As lunchtime approaches, a few cars pull into the Kitchi Gammi parking lot, and I start to feel self-conscious pointing my binoculars straight into a flock of gulls. I am not wholly unsympathetic to people who would never think to examine ring-bills at closer range, and many times I too have considered them annoying or, at best, mildly entertaining. Yet at Kitchi Gammi, I have been alone with them for the past hour, watching them interact undiminished by the human presence that propels them to quarrel over food or call out in alarm. With only the rocks and the sky and waters before me, the gulls have appeared in a more natural setting than I am used to seeing them in.

Before long, two red-breasted mergansers come swimming down the coast, and it is not difficult to give my eyes a respite from the gulls. The two drakes are in breeding plumage. When a loon unexpectedly surfaces near one of them, the startled bird rears up in a flurry, displaying its spectacular-looking green-buffed head, rusty chest, and stark white neck band. There is something deeply dignified, uniquely elegant, and unpretentious about the conduct and bearing of red-breasted mergansers. Though they are large ducks, their neck and body are long and slender, and when feeding, most of their size and splendor are concealed under the water. When not feeding, they move with a swift and regal air, holding their long red bills and wispy head crests high, and when in pairs or groups, they swim close together and dive and surface in rapid succession. In flight along the lakeshore, their slim streamlined bodies hug the water like targeted projectiles. And except around mating season, they are largely silent birds.

Red-breasteds are birds of northern waters. Their North American breeding range spans much of Canada and Alaska and dips into the United States only around the Great Lakes, reaching its southern limit in the Superior region. Like ring-bills, they nest on the ground and favor the shore, rarely venturing into the surrounding forested lake lands. Mothers-to-be conceal their down-lined nests close to the water, usually among dense grasses or shrubs, such as gooseberry or Labrador tea, or under evergreen branches. Hollows among roots and rocks can also do the job. Moreover, unlike the larger common merganser, which nests mainly in tree hollows and also frequents the Superior forest, red-breasteds are able to make use of a range of sites, provided that their nests can be well hidden. They can therefore breed not only on the waters of the boreal forest but also on the lakes, bays, and rivers of the Arctic tundra. All this means that while flocks migrate through the Superior region on their way to and from their breeding grounds, summertime sightings along the Minnesota shore are usually confined to a few occasional birds at any given location. Along the lake's northern coastline, Ontario's bays and inlets provide much more abundant vegetation and shelter than do the bare ledges and outcrops of the Minnesota shore.

Red-breasteds usually arrive on their nesting grounds slightly after ring-bills, some time in late April or, more commonly, May. Pair formation begins in late winter and continues through the spring migration. Like ring-bills, red-breasteds are gregarious birds and can often be seen in flocks, especially on their wintering grounds along shallow coastal bays and estuaries. Where possible, they build their nests in proximity to one another. Yet, in sharp contrast with the shared nest building, incubating, and chick-rearing practices of ring-bills, female red-breasteds assume sole responsibility for all aspects of preparing and caring for the young, though drakes are occasionally spotted with a brood. Young red-breasteds are born fully precocial and capable of feeding independently. Unlike ring-bill chicks, which stay in their nest and hide in nearby vegetation and are fed by their parents until they fledge, red-breasteds need their mother mainly for warmth at night and in stormy weather while still downy. Unfortunately, when it comes to reproductive success, the species' late breeding habits place many chicks at a disadvantage. Hatchlings require two months to fledge, and many fail to grow strong enough to make the arduous fall migration during the short summers that characterize the red-breasted's breeding range. Gulls and other predators also take a large number of young.

Mergansers are excellent divers for small fish and crustaceans. They are commonly called sawbills after the sharp, sawlike ridges on their upper mandible, which enable them to grasp slippery fish. These serrations have also given the red-breasted its particular species name, *serrator,* from the Latin word meaning "to cut or serrate." The term *sawbill,* however, is used more generally to refer to any merganser, be it red-breasted, common, or hooded. The same is true of another popular name, sheldrake, which comes from the shell-like white mottling that appears on the bird's grey sides. As are ring-bills and herring gulls, immature as well as female red-breasteds can be hard to distinguish from common mergansers.

While the Minnesota shore may not provide ideal breeding grounds for sawbills, the bird has given its name to two popular features of the regional landscape, a lake and a road. Sawbill Lake, which has an outfitting post for trips into the Boundary Waters Canoe Area Wilderness, lies about half an hour's drive inland from the shore by way of a one-lane gravel road known as the Sawbill Trail. The trail follows the Temperance River into the Sawtooth Mountains and is a popular scenic drive. A paddle on Sawbill Lake provides many rewards, including a floating bog that lines the northern side of the channel with neighboring Kelso Lake. Steadying my canoe sideways against the glistening border of sphagnum moss, I try to see inside the water-filled leaves of a clump of pitcher plants. The plants' stiff stalks are crowned by large, solitary burgundy flowers that hang upside down, and at their base, the rosette of curved, rainwater-filled leaves provides a deadly trap for unsuspecting insects. Pulling out my field guide, I read that the plant uses both fragrance and color to attract insects, but that apparently some mosquitoes and moths are immune to its digestive enzymes and, once trapped, can live out their lives in the pitchers. Unfortunately, my canoe is too far away to let me see inside the pitchers, and after a brief attempt, I decide against raising myself over its side to get a better look.

During my paddle on Sawbill, Kelso, and Alton Lakes, I pass many small, tree-clad rocky islands. Concealed by shrubs and low-draping branches, the islands' nooks and crannies would seem to offer choice nesting sites for red-breasteds. Common mergansers are frequently sited on the border lakes, yet while renting my canoe at Sawbill Lodge, I was told that no sawbills nest on Sawbill Lake. During the hour I spend eating my lunch on one of the lake's picturesque islets, I count nearly a dozen canoes on the water, hardly a serene environment for a mother with brood.

Sawbills are oft admired birds, and it makes sense that features of the local landscape should be named after them. Lake Superior, however, also has a number of Gull Islands, including one in the Apostle chain and another, which actually consists of a chain of four small islets, northeast of Passage Island off the tip of Isle Royale. Around Superior, many place-names associated with birds and other wildlife originally came from the Ojibwe and usually indicated frequent sightings of a species in a particular area. In a similar fashion, many Gull islands, harbors, bays, bars, motels, and restaurants in coastal areas around the country probably owe their names mainly to the gull's pervasive presence and association with shore life. Yet I like to think that people name places after flora and fauna, as they do after prominent men and women, to convey their admiration and respect, and not only to provide factual information about a species' presence, or former presence as the case may be with sawbills on Sawbill Lake. This is likely to be true for the sawbill. But for the gull, I wonder if it is probably not often the case.

Most people, I think it is safe to conclude, would much rather behold a red-breasted merganser than a ring-billed gull. This is unfortunate but understandable since the latter's abundance and habit of frequenting city parks, parking lots, and other places where there are food scraps to be had have made it seem un-remarkable and undeserving of admiration. Yet, catch a few ring-bills alone in a natural setting, as I have done this morning at Kitchi Gammi, and such a conclusion seems almost unthinkable.

Crosby's Paradox

FEW RIVERS ENTER LAKE SUPERIOR WITH AS MUCH
style as the Manitou, which drops its waters over a ten-foot fall directly into a cove on the Minnesota shore. The waterfall is on private property, and a gate with a no-trespassing sign prevents easy
access to it from Highway 61. Fortunately, thanks to the vision of
George H. Crosby, approximately ten miles of the Manitou River's
gorge, including some impressive stands of virgin cedar and yellow
birch, are open to the public as part of George H. Crosby Manitou
State Park. In January 1954, Crosby donated 3,320 acres to the state
on the condition that the land be used for the establishment of
the park; he had apparently also expressed a desire to see the land
remain undeveloped. Unlike other parks on the Minnesota shore,
Crosby Manitou is designated as a "natural," not a "recreational,"
park, and use is restricted to hiking and backpacking. It has no
visitors' center, no modern restrooms, no RV hookups, and it cannot be accessed from Highway 61. Its entrance is marked only by a
wooden sign off a dirt road, a former logging railroad grade, seven
miles north of the small town of Finland. Primitive and inacces-

sible, nature in its natural state—that was Crosby's vision for the Manitou River gorge.

I admire this vision, and the foresight and generosity it contained. Crosby liked the outdoors and was by many accounts a rugged man. He hiked far and wide on Superior's forested ranges, carrying food and a blanket, sleeping under the stars, and going for days before returning to settled places. Yet there is a paradox, and it is a difficult one for me to swallow. Crosby was no Henry David Thoreau. It is hard to imagine him penning the words "in Wildness is the preservation of the world." Far from it. He hiked Superior's ranges prospecting for iron, and eventually he became a wealthy, turn-of-the-century mining baron. While he may have set aside a small piece of land for future generations, he built his own fortune on nature's back.

Yet what a piece of land it is, a uniquely varied scenery encompassing seven miles of cascading river, ancient lava-born hills and overlooks, steep sandstone bluffs, pristine stands of northern hardwood forest, a small slice of Superior coastline, as well as a spring-fed lake that Crosby described as "probably the most beautiful lake in northern Minnesota." As do many areas around Lake Superior, Crosby Manitou offers a daunting list of impressive sights to choose from. Fortunately, it is possible to take in most of these by following a circular route from the dirt parking lot, past Bensen Lake, to the river's edge, and then back again via the Yellow Birch, River, and Matt Willis trails.

One of the highlights of Crosby Manitou is a 130-acre stand of old-growth yellow birch forest. While yellow birch is common on the southern Superior shore, the Crosby Manitou stand is the only self-perpetuating forest of its kind in Minnesota. Many of the tree trunks are much too large for me to get my arms around, and towering far above me, their canopies offer bare glimpses of the sky beyond. Northern hardwoods, such as yellow birch and sugar maple, favor the deep, rich soils associated with glacial deposits. During the latest glaciation, the lava-born Sawtooth highlands, which parallel the lake from East Beaver Bay north to the Cascade River, blocked the advance of the Superior ice lobe, which left a moraine of sediment and debris along the outer margin of its western flank. In Crosby Manitou and surrounding regions of the Sawtooth range, stands of yellow birch and sugar maple occur mainly as small patches within the larger forest of paper birch, aspen, white spruce, and balsam fir. The Manitou watershed contains exemplary stands and some of the few virgin areas of this forest type in the Great Lakes region. A few miles northwest of the state park, The Nature Conservancy's Upper Manitou Forest Preserve protects an additional 2,000 acres of hardwood forest.

Come September, changing colors march across the Sawtooths like floats in a ticker-tape parade, and the Fall Color Tour draws cars onto the graveled back roads of the Superior forest. The sugar maple dominates the Sawtooth hardwood forest, and its brilliant display easily steals the show, reminding me of New England falls. Rich canopies of orange and red envelop the forest in a womb of warm colors, creating a storybook environment of magical, filtered sunlight and soft, leaf-carpeted grounds. Sugar maples rely on the proximity of lake-warmed air to keep winter temperatures above minus forty degrees, at which point their sap freezes, and favor southern slopes, which receive more sunshine and are more sheltered from wind than their northern counterparts. Moist loamy soils, the kind sugar maple and yellow birch saplings need, are created by a generous annual infusion of nutrient-rich leaf litter as well as by wind-strewn debris that comes to rest on the slopes.

Unlike in the remainder of the Sawtooths, in the upland terrain between Bensen Lake and the Manitou River, yellow birch and white cedar are codominant in the hardwood forest, with sugar maple appearing as a subordinate species alongside white spruce, balsam fir, and heartleaf and paper birch. A long-lived tree that grows slowly, yellow birch often lives at least 150 to 200 years and does not begin to produce seed until its fourth decade, with optimal production usually occurring a few decades later. Yet it produces fairly frequent bumper crops of wind-borne seeds, which germinate on downed logs, rotting stumps, and mossy, humus-rich soils where windthrows have opened up the canopy to light. Except in the case of very old trees, whose trunks become a grooved reddish brown, yellow birch is easily identified by its lustrous bronze bark, which peels off into small, slender strips. Because its bark is thin, the tree is vulnerable to being killed by fire, and its predominance in the forest is associated with the absence of a severe blaze for a good century and a half or more. The same can be said of white cedar, which while it grows well on rocky uplands, is often confined to less fire-prone moist lowlands. Yet mature stands of large hardwoods, including both yellow birch and sugar maple, tend to be less vulnerable to fire than conifers. Both the intensity and the spread of flames are reduced by deep, moist soils and dense shade, the latter limiting understory growth and the accumulation of fuel loads.

Leaving the upland forest, the trail descends a steep sandstone bluff to arrive at the river's bank. Upstream, one of many gently sloping falls lining the lower river, this one aptly named the Crosby cascades, has formed where the water flows over erosion-resistant diabase lava rock. At the top of the cascade, the swollen current has almost obscured a large boulder that in times of lower water provides an excellent platform for studying the Manitou's tumbling course. *Manitou* is an Ojibwe word for "Spirit," and shielding my face against the spray, I can easily understand how native people came to name the river after the swirling, spiritlike mists of white water that ascend with the wind. I think it fortunate that Crosby chose to honor the native connection with the river by incorporating the Ojibwe reference into the park's name. Personally, I would have preferred simply Manitou River State Park.

One evening in June 1886, Crosby reportedly came home and told his wife, "I quit my job. I'm going to look for ore on the Mesabi." The forested northern Minnesota frontier had yet to close, and the first shipment of ore, from the Soudan mine on the Vermilion Range, had taken place only two years earlier. Prospecting was not for the lazy or risk averse, and Crosby was but one of many young and adventuresome would-be mining magnates. Originally from Hastings, Minnesota, he had tried his hand at a laundry list of conventional trades before he turned to prospecting, including grocer's clerk, plumber's assistant, salesman, and real estate agent. He seized a remote chance at fortune and reaped the rewards. Yet even after having struck ore many times over, he maintained an eclectic range of pursuits. He expanded his mining ventures to the American Southwest, financed development and served on the boards of civic associations in Duluth, ran an experimental farm and a luxury resort on his Serpent Lake property, and opened a car repair and service shop.

Crosby discovered several ore bodies on the Mesabi Range, including the large Hawkins mine, his first, in 1903. But it was to the development of the Cuyuna, the last of Minnesota's three ranges to be developed, that much of his life was devoted. As elsewhere, the presence of ore on the Cuyuna had long been suspected before the first discovery was made. A federal land survey team had reported magnetic anomalies in the area in 1869, and in 1865 the first state geological survey report confirming the existence of mineral deposits in northeastern Minnesota was published. The 1850s had seen brief, but intense, prospecting for copper on the north shore, stimulated by the opening up of the region to white settlement under the 1854 Treaty of La Pointe. As a historical marker along Highway 61 explains, Clifton, the first town on the Minnesota shore, was platted in 1855 near the mouth of the French River, where copper traces had first been discovered in the 1840s. Prospectors soon swarmed the area like flies, and tent towns sprang up near the mouths of the Knife and other major rivers. Mineral discoveries on the shore, however, proved disappointing, and by the decade's end, having barely been platted, Clifton and other towns disappeared. Prospectors turned their attention inland, to iron discoveries on the ranges west of the lake.

In 1904, the Illinois-born Cuyler Adams, who had begun drilling on the Cuyuna after observing compass deflections while surveying his property in Deerwood, hit ore. The new iron range was called the Cuyuna, in honor of the man whose discoveries lay behind it and his large Saint Bernard dog, Una. Shortly after Adams struck ore, Crosby arrived on the Cuyuna, where he discovered several new mines and founded the town that bears his name. In an interesting side note, unlike the ore on Minnesota's other ranges, the Cuyuna's iron contained manganese, and at the federal government's request, the range supplied almost all of the mineral used to manufacture U.S. munitions in World War I. Unfortunately for Crosby, processing the manganese was expensive and turned out to be a money-losing proposition, and it was not until the 1950s, after a long legal battle over the government's failure to honor its commitment to indemnify producers against loss, that he was finally repaid a portion of his wartime debt.

On October 5, 1909, the town of Crosby was platted in the heart of the Cuyuna Range. Crosby had bought the land for the town and carefully planned the location and layout of its homes and businesses. In a 1913 promotional booklet titled *Crosby: The Metropolis of the Cuyuna Range,* he proudly described his new settlement as a "city built to a plan." In the town of Crosby, he noted, the sidewalks had been cemented from the start, even the smallest cottages had been given water, electric, and sewer connections, and to avoid monotony, the buildings had been designed in different styles and colors. "You come to no rude mining camp when you move to Crosby," he ensured prospective settlers. The town, Crosby liked to point out, had been built for permanence. Unlike many other mining settlements, which often had to be moved when drilling turned up ore under their buildings, its land had been thoroughly prospected before construction began. The town grew quickly. By 1914, it had become the largest settlement on the Cuyuna Range, boasting a population of about three thousand, which is slightly more than it does today. For Crosby the man, it turned out to be a good investment.

As such, it was hardly unique. While squatter settlements sprouted abundantly on the copper and iron ranges around the lake, in areas where mining was productive and a steady labor force was required, it was common for companies and investors to build and plat towns whose houses were then leased to miners. Town construction ventures were a lucrative business, and as such, attracted speculators intent on turning quick profits. Many mining towns were characterized by inexpensive, dilapidated buildings and filthy environs, but a few were planned with the specific intent of drawing a stable, high-quality workforce. Like Crosby, the town of Coleraine, constructed by the Oliver Mining Company on the Mesabi Range, contained attractive homes in a variety of designs and colors, generous but affordable lots, as well as good schools, roads, and public amenities. Yet, unlike the Mesabi, the Cuyuna already had several sizable settlements by the time mining took off, and there was less need for new town construction. Crosby's foresight was to get into not only the mining but also the building business on the Cuyuna early on.

While it would be an exaggeration to say that in planning his town he was motivated only by a concern for the welfare of prospective miners, Crosby was known to be scrupulously honest and civic-minded to a fault, and in all probability he wanted to do more than make a profit. The impression one gets of Crosby is that of an apparently ambitious man who aspired to leave a mark for posterity—after all, despite wanting to avoid publicity in association with his land grant to the state, he stuck his name to both a park and a town—but who also planned for the future and held strong commitments to the places he invested and believed in. The fact that he no doubt wanted the town to reflect positively on his name and may have been steeped in turn-of-the-century corporate paternalism does not make his devotion to its prosperity any less genuine. Long after mining had begun to decline and he himself had become comfortably established, he continued to spend his summers at his Serpent Lake property and to tirelessly promote tourism and business on the range. I try to put myself in the shoes of the early miners, full of their dreams, who came to the empty town. They were the ordinary people who staked their futures on men like Crosby. For them, he was not such a bad bet.

Yet for those who wanted to protect the rapidly vanishing American wilderness, men like Crosby were a different ilk. Influenced by the writings and ideas of Thoreau, John Muir, Jack London, and the work of the Izaak Walton League and other conservation advocates, the seeds of environmental consciousness had been slowly stirring across the country. In contrast to environmentalists' concerns over heavy industry and resource exploitation, Crosby held an altogether positive outlook on the rapidly changing relationship between nature and development. He supported the construction of loading docks at Duluth, Two Harbors, and Silver Bay, urged tax relief for mining companies, and helped to fund the power survey of the Saint Louis River that paved the way for Jay Cooke's establishment of the hydroelectric dam at Thomson. Since the mining industry depended on shipping to carry its ore to eastern steel mills, he was also an early proponent of expanding the system of locks, canals, and lighthouses on the Great Lakes and lobbied for decades to promote the construction of a deepwater passage through the Saint Lawrence River. Complications in the negotiations between the United States and Canada, as well as in the Senate treaty ratification process, prevented the Saint Lawrence Seaway project from being completed until 1959, by which time both Crosby and the Great Lakes mining industry were well past their prime. Nevertheless, by enabling ocean-going freighters to reach Lake Superior, the seaway enabled Duluth to become the country's largest inland port, something that Crosby as well as Cooke favored.

As for recreational development and tourism on the north shore, Crosby would, I believe, have agreed with the message on a Duluth billboard, "Tourism. It's working." Tourism followed closely upon the turn-of-the-century extension of railroad and steamship service around the lake. On the Minnesota shore, it made rapid inroads with the completion of Highway 61 from Duluth to the Canadian border in 1924, of which Crosby was an outspoken proponent. Were it not for the decision to restrict development, Crosby Manitou might have become, as Conservation

Commissioner Chester Wilson stated it would in early 1954, one of the most popular parks in the state, evolving not unlike many other recreational destinations on the north shore.

As their popularity has increased, the eight state parks that lie on the north shore, from Gooseberry Falls in the south to Grand Portage in the north, have built and expanded their visitors' centers, parking lots, campgrounds, and other facilities. Visitors that come to hike, camp, canoe, fish, ski, and otherwise enjoy the parks, as well as surrounding state and federal lands, support an ever expanding corridor of restaurants, motels, gas stations, and gift shops along Highway 61. Unable to safely accommodate seasonal and weekend surges in recreational traffic, as well as the steady flow of trucks between Duluth and Thunder Bay, Ontario, the highway is in the midst of a decades' long expansion project. Every summer more trees are felled to make way for new pavement.

The Minnesota shore is a strangely disjointed place. I cannot help but think that Crosby would have had a more optimistic view than I do of its present-day mix of industry and development, on the one hand, and state parks and protected natural areas, on the other. For me, the dearth of anything but small parcels of natural sanctity is made all the more lamentable by the startling appeal of the lava-born rocks and lakeside vistas. With most of the shore in private hands, state parks often afford the only public access to the lake. Yet even within their borders, losing myself to the landscape sometimes requires nothing less than a willful act of denying my surroundings, tuning out the drone of highway traffic and closing my eyes to people that pack the trails in the summertime. Lying as it does at the intersection of nature and civilization, the shore attempts to span horizons that are all but impossible to bridge, tantalizing yet also coming up short. No matter how visually stunning, a crowded landscape rarely feels pristine.

I say this despite the fact that I will never completely shed my East Coast origins, and that compared to the mega road networks, brash resorts, and steaming factories of the Atlantic shoreline, this part of the country still has a way of winning over those who want a balance between nature and development, however rough and unsatisfactory it may be. When the pavement ends and I turn my tires onto the dirt road north of Finland only a few miles from highway hotels and gift shops, I am reminded that it is possible to make my peace with this landscape, to stop looking for what it cannot offer in order to see more clearly all that it can. As houses and road signs vanish in the clouds of dust that fill my rearview mirror, the forested slopes of the Sawtooth range rise through the windshield.

A slender string of bog land surrounds the road heading into the Manitou landscape, and just where the small wooden sign points to the turnoff for the park, the scenery opens up on a post-card north-woods image—a small lake surrounded by forested hillsides and, at its far end, a black spruce and tamarack bog. The sugar maples may steal the fall color show in the Sawtooths, but weeks after they have turned, the tamaracks infuse the bogs along the Superior forest back roads with warm tones, their needles changing from deep green to rich saffron before dropping to the ground. With winter close at hand and the rest of the landscape already caught in the postpartum brooding of November's dreary clasp, the bronze, gold, and copper shades of bog heaths, mosses, and tamaracks provide a comfortable, if still lively, turning down of the visual scale.

Crosby died in 1961 at the age of ninety-six, the last of Minnesota's great prospectors to pass. His wife and two children had preceded him in death, and while longevity seems to have run in the family—his mother was Duluth's oldest resident when she died a week short of her 103d birthday—Crosby credited the fresh air of the Iron Range for his long life. I have sometimes wondered whether there was a tinge of regret at having lived to see a once pristine landscape transformed by the mining and development that he had helped to promote behind his decision to give a piece of land back to the northern areas that he so loved. In the end, all that matters is that thanks to his vision, a small slice of the Manitou River gorge and the surrounding old-growth northern hardwood forest has been preserved for future generations, of-fering one of the few remaining places on the Minnesota shore where it is still possible to have a wilderness experience.

Bicknell's Geranium

BICKNELL'S GERANIUM IS A SMALL, GROUND-HUGGING plant with light purple flowers and deeply cleft, delicately pointed leaves. It needs dry soil and sunshine and grows best in clearings and open woods. In places where it is not frequently seen, such as the shady northern pine forest, it may appear after a fire or other major disturbance. On July 4, 1999, a powerful windstorm swept through the Boundary Waters Canoe Area Wilderness in northeastern Minnesota. Hiking the Caribou Rock Trail north toward the Canadian border the following summer, I encountered large snags of uprooted brush, requiring frequent detours, and red pine trunks angled precariously from where they snapped a dozen feet off the ground. Seeing a much-liked landscape reduced to rubble can be devastating. The pre-storm scenery survives in memory, but I know that in my lifetime the trail will never look the same. It is no small comfort to see two Bicknell's rising from the sun-warmed soils along the trail, to know that such a pretty little flower has been waiting for one of nature's recurring ravages to unfold its beauty.

Growing close to each of the Bicknell's along the trail is another attractive floral ephemeral, pale or pink corydalis. A larger, shrubbier plant with long slender stems, finely curved bluish leaves, and drooping pink, yellow-tipped flowers, pale corydalis is, like Bicknell's, well adapted to take advantage of a sudden disturbance in the forest. The dormant seeds of both flowers are long-lived and lie deep enough underground to be insulated from the intense heat of flames and severe winds or other upheaval. Yet they are still close enough to the surface to benefit from the rise in soil temperatures caused by a fire or, as along the Caribou Rock Trail, by the removal of shade-providing trees and can make quick use of the changed soil and light conditions. Both Bicknell's and pale corydalis grow best in sunshine, however, and neither is likely to survive for more than a few years after a disturbance. As shrubs and saplings begin to take hold, they and other sun-loving ephemerals will gradually disappear.

Bicknell's geranium was named after Eugene P. Bicknell, a late-nineteenth-century amateur naturalist who birded and collected plants in the Catskill Mountains of New York. On one of his walks, Bicknell saw a small, unfamiliar plant. He sent the specimen, which apparently was not in bloom, to the New York Botanical Garden, where it was named after him by the garden's first director, botanist Nathaniel Lord Britton. Bicknell's name, however, is probably more commonly associated with a previously unknown thrush that he discovered nesting in the Catskill's higher-elevation spruce and fir forests.

Bicknell's is one of more than two hundred species of wild geraniums. Yet it is one of only three species native to the United States, the rest having been introduced from Europe during the country's settlement. Wild geraniums belong to a different genus than cultivated geraniums, which originally came from South Africa. Just as Bicknell's thrush was long believed to be a subspecies of the gray-cheeked thrush, African or cultivated geraniums were thought to belong to the same genus as wild geraniums until the late 1780s, when it was discovered that their petals differed.

Like other wild geraniums, Bicknell's is often called a cranesbill because its long seed case resembles a crane's beak; the name *geranium* comes from the Greek word *geranion*, or "crane."

It was through studying wild geraniums that German botanist and theologian Christian Konrad Sprengel came up with his theory of cross-pollination and reproduction in flowers. Insects, Sprengel observed, are attracted to the color of a flower's nectaries and transport pollen from the stamen, or male organ, of one flower to the pistil, or female organ, of another. He also noticed that some flowers depend not on insects but on wind to disperse their pollen. Sprengel recorded his observations in the book *The Newly Revealed Mystery of Nature in the Structure and Fertilization of Flowers,* published in 1793. The book was widely ignored until the early 1840s, when it was picked up by none other than Charles Darwin, who used it as a basis for his own research on flowers.

The Caribou Rock Trail lies within the hardest hit area of the July 4th blowdown, a long and narrow corridor that stretches along the Canadian border northwest of the town of Grand Marais. Straight-line winds of over ninety miles an hour caused more than 70 percent of the trees in the area to be downed. The devastation is particularly severe on hilltops, where scattered white pines are often the only trees left standing. The damage is less noticeable along the lakeshores where the sun-loving red pines dominate. I later read that constant exposure to off-lake winds may have helped these trees to grow stronger than their more sheltered inland counterparts and thus to survive the storm.

Accessed just two miles off the Gunflint Trail on County Road 65, I can think of few better places than the Caribou Rock Trail to experience, by way of a day hike, the immensity of the pristine, lake-studded Boundary Waters landscape. Valley creek beds are dappled in orange spotted touch-me-nots, and from the bearberry-clad granite ledges high above, an award-winning portfolio of pine-framed vistas unfolds. The lakes below are long and narrow, occupying valleys running southwesterly that were carved from softer bedrock by the glaciers. The trail is a strenuous seven-mile round-trip from the small gravel parking lot to the turnaround at Rose Lake, on the Minnesota-Ontario border. The scenery more than compensates for the absence of long stretches of level ground, but it does not take long for the steep ups and downs to begin to wear on my knees and ankles.

The Caribou Rock Trail straddles the border of the Boundary Waters, with its first half mile located outside the protected wilderness area. While I sit on a rock, soaking my feet in Bearskin Lake, a pontoon boat plies the far end of the water, and a dozen feet to my right, two families unload their four canoes for the short portage to Duncan Lake. Federal regulations protecting the Boundary Waters date to 1926, when northern parts of the Superior National Forest, created in 1909, were set aside for canoe and wilderness recreation. In 1930 Congress passed the Shipstead-Newton-Nolan Act, limiting logging and dam construction around area lakes, and in 1938 the U.S. Forest Service created the Superior Roadless Primitive Areas. Later, Congress authorized funds for the federal government to buy out privately held lands that impaired the area's wilderness character, and a presidential order banned floatplanes, which had been used to ferry people to fly-in resorts.

The growing federal restrictions on land and water use in northeastern Minnesota had been prompted mainly by the lobbying of outdoor enthusiasts and environmental organizations. They were opposed by many local residents, including politicians on the Cook County Board of Commissioners and property and resort owners, who saw the restrictions as a threat to the area's tax base, as well as their own livelihoods. Despite repeated local protests, the Boundary Waters was included in the 1964 National Wilderness Act, introduced by Minnesota Senator Hubert Humphrey, though compromise language exempted the wilderness from several restrictions on logging and road construction. In 1978, the Boundary Waters Canoe Area Wilderness (BWCAW) Act granted approximately one million acres of the border lakes region official wilderness designation and expanded restrictions on logging, which was completely prohibited, motorized use, and mineral exploration.

Yet controversy over the implementation of federal restrictions, especially on motorboats, motorized portages, and floatplanes, has remained, fueling the sentiments of environmentalists and local residents, as well as national organizations and political leaders.

The Boundary Waters preserves the largest area of old-growth forest in the country east of the Rockies. As are Bicknell's geranium and pale corydalis, the jack, red, and white pines that dominate the forest are genetically programmed to take advantage of disturbance, and especially of fire, for reproduction. All three pine species benefit from fire to a greater or lesser extent because it weeds out old and weak trees and restores the relatively open environment in which their saplings grow best. Fire eliminates species that, unlike the pines, are capable of reproducing in the shady understory. The latter include spruce and fir but also, in older mixed stands, maple, yellow birch, basswood, and other hardwoods. While unable to grow on the dry, infertile soils that characterize young jack and red pine stands, hardwoods begin to gain a foothold as the needle-laden ground cover slowly decomposes and a richer organic substratum emerges. Intermittent blazes also reduce the amount of downed logs and shrubs on the ground, making it less likely that future fires will have enough kindling to develop into devastating crown blazes.

Each pine species displays a slightly different postfire regeneration strategy. Jack pine, which often grows in nearly pure stands on dry, southern slopes and thin-soiled rocky ridges and outcrops, is the shortest lived and most fire dependent of the three. It produces relatively open stands, and the assorted shrubs and flowers that grow in its understory, such as mountain maple, bush honeysuckle, and blueberry, are easily eliminated by surface burns. Growing on exposed, arid sites, the stands are vulnerable to lightning strikes and to the rapid spread of wind-driven flames, both of which contribute to high-intensity blazes. Jack pines are usually killed by crown fires, yet their resin-sealed cones open in high temperatures and release heat-resistant seeds that germinate quickly in the charred duff. Its rapid growth and early reproductive maturity enable jack pine to use postfire seed germination to sustain itself.

Red pine is more capable of surviving fire than jack pine, thanks largely to its thicker bark. Yet, it matures slowly and is unable to seed in on ash, relying on intermittent blazes mainly to create the sunny clearings in which its seeds germinate best. Red pines are found mainly along lakeshores and on islands, which offer some protection from extreme fires. Like the red pine, the white pine relies on periodic bumper crops of seed from nearby stands, which thus must contain a sufficient number of mature trees, to ensure postfire regeneration. Able to grow in moister soils and to reproduce in greater shade than either of the other two pines, it is often found in stands on north-facing slopes and in valleys in the Boundary Waters area and as an understory species in the northern hardwood forest on the Sawtooth range.

While nature provided the winds that downed the trees along the Caribou Rock Trail, decades of human fire suppression have left the forest vulnerable to devastation. The presettlement pine forest sustained itself through intermittent fire, and in its absence old and weak trees, which are especially susceptible to windthrow, have been left standing. Fire suppression policies followed in the wake of logging, and early clear-cuts eliminated many mature, seed-bearing red and white pines and enabled fast-growing competitors, such as aspen, to colonize clearings. Turn-of-the-century loggers generally spared saplings and small pines, which grew to tower like flagpoles over the younger regrowth, becoming especially vulnerable to windthrow. The same vulnerability confronts species such as fir and spruce, which in the absence of fire have come to dominate large parts of the former pine forest. Spruce budworm infestations have weakened both species but especially the fir, despite what the name suggests. Shaped by human intervention of one sort or another, today's forest looks much different than it did a century ago.

Of all the pines, the white pine was the most extensively logged and has been the slowest to recover. Efforts to restore the species to even a sliver of its former range date to the early postlogging period, when extensive planting of seedlings was undertaken by the depression-era Civilian Conservation Corps. Yet white pines face many challenges, and at times the obstacles have appeared to overwhelm the possible benefits of trying to regenerate them. Old-growth stands, with an ample supply of seed-bearing trees, are concentrated mainly in the Boundary Waters, while only scattered patches remain on Superior National Forest and other public lands. The white pine generally fares poorer in cool, damp northern environments than does either the jack or red pine. It requires longer growing seasons and easily becomes susceptible to the fungal disease white-pine blister rust, which has infested extensive stands of the tree in northeastern Minnesota. A few miles north of Tofte on the Sawbill Trail, the U.S. Forest Service is testing a rust-resistant variety of the tree, but even if such efforts prove successful, white pine regeneration will remain a labor-intensive task. Lower branches need to be pruned to protect against the spread of blister rust, buds need to be capped against white pine weevil infestations, which kill new growth at the tree's top, and saplings need to be fenced against the relentless browsing of white-tailed deer. Present labors will bear fruit mainly for generations to come. In the meantime, not only the white pine but also the human bond with the natural forest is being restored.

One year after the windstorm, scattered clumps of fireweed have already moved into sun-filled clearings along the Caribou Rock Trail. As do Bicknell's geranium and pale corydalis, fireweed colonizes disturbed areas, and as its name suggests, often becomes ubiquitous in the wake of a burn, its lightweight seeds arriving quickly by wind from noncharred sites nearby. Fire suppression has restricted the growth not only of pines but also of these and other sun-loving ephemerals, such as ox-eye daisy, pearly everlasting, thistles, and white campions, whose flowers attract a lively flurry of birds, bees, and butterflies to clearings in the forest. Few of these flowers will remain for more than a couple of years after a disturbance, yet during their brief existence, they will have performed an important function in the initial phase of post-disturbance forest regeneration. Their decomposed litter cycles nutrients into the ground, and their network of roots helps to improve the moisture retention ability of the soil, making it easier for shrubs and tree saplings to take hold.

In the absence of seed-bearing white and red pines, the next phase of colonizers will consist mainly of sun-loving species such as aspen, whose root suckers can easily grow by several feet per season on moister sites, and jack pine, which has few competitors on poor, dry soils. Already, some parts of the trail require what could almost qualify as bushwhacking through dense regrowth of chin-height aspen and mountain maple. Yet like the flowers that preceded them, these short-lived trees are unable to reproduce in their own shade, and in the absence of another disturbance, they will usually disappear within a century, having been gradually replaced in the forest by less light-demanding species such as fir, spruce, and birch.

Nature, however, can be counted on to work its logic of ruin and renewal in cycles. With so much downed material and so little shade cover to keep it moist, sooner or later fire will probably come to the post-blowdown forest. Unimpeded by dense forest canopies, winds will spread the flames quickly. Present plans call for using prescribed burns, which have previously been prohibited in the Boundary Waters, to reduce fuel loads as well as for allowing natural fires that do not threaten private property to burn themselves out. Having once been removed, fire will likely be gradually reintroduced as a determinant of Boundary Waters forest ecology, though in a strictly regulated fashion. For many areas of the Superior forest, where seed-bearing red and white pines are too few or far-removed, fire will probably come too late. For the pine stands that survived the blowdown around the Caribou Rock Trail, however, there may fortunately still be some hope.

To see devastation descend on an area once in one's lifetime is enough, and I do not relish the thought of another disturbance crossing this part of the forest, of losing again the familiar contours of some of my favorite natural places. If fire does come to this part of the border area in my lifetime, I will hold on to the hope of once again seeing Bicknell's geranium and other small floral ephemerals rising from sunny clearings along the trail. For all the loss, there is, the windstorm of July 4 has taught me, an instinctual pleasure in seeing the varied and rapidly changing habitats a recovering landscape holds. How forgiving and full of contagious hope nature feels in such a place.

No Bar River

THE RIVER WAS NAMED TEMPERANCE, A PARK SIGN used to explain, because it has no sandbar at its mouth. Most rivers on Lake Superior's Minnesota shore cut their channels through basalt and other lavas. Compared with rivers that cross more easily eroded sandstones and shales, they have fairly light sediment loads and produce few of the sandy bays found elsewhere around the lake. The Temperance apparently carries an even lighter sediment load than other north shore rivers, and the deep waters at its mouth have traditionally prevented enough sand and gravel from building up to form a bar. The park sign, however, made no attempt to explain why the river was named Temperance simply because it has no bar. This, it is assumed, should be self-evident. The old sign came down a few years ago, and the new sign does not mention the source of the river's name. This seems fitting since the No Bar River, in many seasons, now sports a bar.

When the river was first included in the state geological survey of 1848–52, it was called the *Kawimbash,* a name that apparently came from the Ojibwe word for "deep hollow." The name

Temperance first appears in a mid-1860s survey report, which refers to the river as the "No Bar or Temperance River." The temperance movement emerged in Minnesota, as in other parts of the country, around mid-century, seeking to ban saloons or bars and prohibit the sale of alcohol to new settlers as well as Native Americans. The pre-state territorial legislature had outlawed both the manufacture of liquor and its sale to the Indians, and the 1854 Treaty of La Pointe with the Ojibwe had banned alcohol on the Grand Portage and Fond du Lac reservations. Among European settlers, abstinence associations, such as the Sons of Temperance, emerged during the latter decades of the century. The river's name is a geological pun, I later read in a book, wondering if I am the only one who did not initially get it.

With its headwaters in the Boundary Waters Canoe Area Wilderness, the Temperance River runs a twenty-odd-mile course through forested, bog-filled terrains before entering a narrow gorge to meet the lake. Its watershed is one of the largest on the north shore and takes in a large swath of the Sawtooth range. The mountains' sawtooth-like appearance, which is especially noticeable from Grand Marais, is the result of varied rates of erosion between different lava flows and silts and minor sedimentary deposits, which has produced steep northern ridges and gently inclining southern slopes. As a roadside marker just south of Grand Marais explains, the 1.1-billion-year-old basalt flows that underlie the mountains and shape the coast were not the result of continuous volcanism. During long pauses between eruptions, rivers carried eroded sediments toward the Superior basin, leaving deposits of sandstone and shale that over subsequent millennia were more prone to weathering and erosion than the surrounding lava rocks.

The magnitude of tectonic activity associated with the mid-continental rift period is mind-boggling, especially when viewed against the comparatively quiescent ten-thousand-year time span during which humans have lived around the lake. The eruptions, it is believed, lasted on and off for about twenty million years, covering the land thousands of feet thick with hundreds of separate flows. The lava welled up through cracks that appeared in the earth's crust as the North American continent pulled apart along a great rift, some fifty to a hundred miles wide, that arched from lower Michigan through the Superior basin south to Kansas. Had the rifting not inexplicably stopped, the expanding basin might have left in place of today's lake the fabled China seas that Samuel de Champlain and other early explorers hoped to discover.

Following the Cauldron Trail up the Temperance River gorge, it is difficult to decide which of nature's forces has left the greatest imprint on the shore. Placards along the trail explain that nine thousand years ago torrential, postglacial meltwaters ripped large chunks from the river's channel, and pebbles and boulders, caught in the swirling waters, ground huge cauldrons out of the bedrock. Once the meltwaters began to recede, the Temperance cut progressively deeper into the bedrock to keep up with the lake's falling level. Thousands of years later, erosion continues to change the face of the gorge as seasonal floodwaters work their force on joints and weak points in the river's channel. Exposed bedrock near the top of a waterfall is especially vulnerable, and each time a chunk breaks off, the rock behind it faces greater erosion. Over time, chunk after chunk falls away, causing the waterfall to migrate slowly upstream.

When I visit Temperance River State Park, I am usually happy to leave other people to explore the river gorge and to spend my time down by the lakeshore. In spite of its no-bar name, the Temperance River sometimes sports a quite sizable sandbar at its mouth. Most north shore rivers, especially those with small watersheds that contain few lakes and bogs in which to store excess runoff, have fairly large seasonal, and sometimes even weekly or daily, fluctuations in their flows. Their sandbars are repeatedly inundated and undercut by torrents of spring meltwater that wash their sediments back out into the lake. The Temperance has a larger watershed than most rivers on the Minnesota shore, yet it still experiences significant fluctuations in its flows, and its bar is at great risk for being eroded by waters forcing their way through the narrow, rock-lined outlet. During the past few years, however, changing precipitation patterns, especially reduced amounts of snowfall, have decreased the force and volume of runoff, making it less likely that gravels accumulated at the river's mouth will be swept away in spring.

Changes in the strength and direction of waves due to storms and seasonal variations in wind patterns also have a significant impact on the scene at the river's mouth, alternately building up and undercutting bars and beaches. So do fluctuations in Great Lakes' water levels. Following highs in the mid-1980s and, to a lesser extent, mid-1990s, the water level in Lake Superior has been falling, reaching lows not recorded since the mid-1960s. Declining precipitation rates and increased surface evaporation, the latter brought on by reduced ice cover during milder winters and by warmer summers, are both to blame. The lower the lake level, the more shoreline is exposed, and the less accumulated sand and gravel it takes for a bar to break the water's surface. Changing water levels are of concern to many, scientists and port authorities alike, and their causes, whether mainly natural or human-generated climactic fluctuation, are still being debated.

This having been said, the Temperance River received its no-bar name for a good reason. Historically, it was less prone to bar formation than other north shore rivers, and until a few decades ago, the water of its mouth was deep enough to serve as a safe harbor for small boats. Much of the sediment needed to form a bar comes from the river, which deposits and over the years stores eroded sands and gravels on the lake bottom some distance from land. Given the traditionally light sediment loads of the Temperance, the waves and currents that move sands from the lake bottom toward shore, building up bars and beaches, have had relatively little to work with. Moreover, the river's mouth is unusually deep, requiring the accumulation of a good deal of sediment before a bar becomes visible above the water. Reduced spring runoff and other factors may have increased the prospects for bar formation at the mouth of the Temperance, but they offer little in the way of a guarantee.

Along the Temperance shore, the bar or no-bar status of the river's mouth is not the only phenomenon worth investigating. Southwest of the river's mouth, there is an unusual stretch of rock, one of the few places on the shore where the basalt is not dark and angular but fairly smooth and light-colored, more oxygenated and iron-rich. Sensuous curves of water-worn flows incline gently toward the lake, and from the vantage point of an outcrop just beyond the beach of the lower campground, half a dozen small undulations of rock extend like smooth, contorted fingers atop the wet sands.

The flows tend toward violet gray and brown, but when wet by rain or lake spray, they take on the luscious shades of burgundy wine and chocolate. It is on clear days in early summer that the ledges are at their best, however, when the ice is gone, the rocks' surface dry, and the sun's glow still soft and magical. On rare days when these conditions are present, the ledges assume the delicate casts of rose-tinted ivory and of a pale creamy tan. Nowhere else have I seen such heavenly basalt, and the moment it comes into view, the desire to hike on drains out of me like water in a sieve.

The basalt outcrops on the Temperance shore offer what must be one of the best displays of mineral-filled cavities, or amygdules, around the lake. Decorative chips of white calcite and more uncommon pale green and pink minerals fill small pockets in the rock. Basalt is a fluid lava and cools quickly as it flows onto the surface of the earth. During the cooling process, gas bubbles made their way from the center of the flows toward their upper layers, which were cooler as a result of being in closer contact with the air. Where the bubbles became trapped, they left cavities in the basalt. Hot groundwater associated with later burial of the lava flows eventually percolated through the rock, depositing dissolved minerals in the cavities, as well as in veins and cracks.

By the time the last glaciers retreated from the Superior basin some ten thousand years ago, the repeated weight, grinding, and internal freezing and thawing of successive ice sheets had eroded and cracked and crushed vast quantities of the basalt, leaving only the modest highlands that parallel the shore today. Solid lava layers, in which amygdules were lodged, broke into chunks that fractured into ever smaller pieces, whose surfaces were later smoothed by the turbulence of postglacial meltwaters. The pebbles, many with mineral-filled cavities, continue to be carried ashore by powerful lake waves.

Most amygdaloidal pebbles on the Temperance beach are dominated by the brown or blue gray shade of basalt, or the orange tint of rhyolite, another midcontinental rift lava rock, their surfaces adorned by random globular designs of white or tan calcite, green chlorite or epidote, and other minerals. Where many pebbles have amygdules, some have only holes, or vesicles. The holes may once have contained minerals, which were later plucked by the glaciers or eroded away by waves. Or if the gas bubbles that formed them became caught in places where thick, impermeable layers of rock prevented solutions from permeating, they may never have had any minerals.

Amygdaloidal pebbles are easily found on many parts of the north shore. Yet chancing on a Lake Superior agate or other highly prized amygdule is usually rare. In the case of agates, waters rich in quartz leached in from surrounding areas and percolated through the basalt over a considerable span of time. Each new trickle or flow added another band to a concentric ring of already crystallized layers, whose color and texture varied depending on the water's temperature and mineral composition. The bands accreted inward from the outside wall and often, but not always, filled the cavity. Lake Superior's agates are believed to be among the oldest in the world, having formed within the 1.1-billion-year-old rift lavas. They are especially known for their intense red and orange color, which comes from the presence of hematite, a mineral that forms when iron is exposed to oxygen and "rusts." Since basalt is rich in iron, waters that percolated through its layers or seeped in from surrounding lava-born soils left high concentrations of iron in the cavities. The colors of an agate vary depending on the amount of iron and the degree of oxidation its bands were exposed to. Since iron oxidizes only when exposed to air, once formed, the agates had to be released from their rocky bondage before assuming their distinctive colors. Some of this was the work of the glaciers, which crushed the surrounding basalt and freed the agates, but glaciation was also preceded by a billion years of erosion and weathering.

On Michigan's copper-rich Keweenaw Peninsula, extensive layers of eroded sands and sediments settled on the basalt floors during long interruptions in the volcanism. Not only iron, but also copper-rich solutions later filled vesicles and veins in the basalt, and also penetrated minute spaces between sands and pebbles in the more permeable sandstone and conglomerate layers. Copper solutions also became concentrated in large masses in veins and other empty spaces in the bedrock. Unlike agates, which tended mainly to crack and break during glacial transport, the soft native copper was malleable enough to be bent, flattened, and otherwise reshaped. Pieces of "float copper," having been dislodged from the bedrock and carried, or "floated," as far south as Ohio and Indiana by the glaciers, display a wide range of shapes and sizes, from tiny specks to huge boulders weighing several tons. Today, there is a much better chance of finding an agate than a piece of float copper around the lake, and both are most likely to be found after storm waves have reconfigured the assortment of pebbles and debris on the shore, or swollen rivers have upturned and carried sediments downstream.

Compared to such infrequent finds, seeing a bar at the mouth of the Temperance River seems to be a fairly safe bet. This, at least, has been my thinking in recent years, when the presence of sizable sandbars has made the river's name appear to have become somewhat of a misnomer. When first coined, the name *Temperance* may have been an apt geological, to say nothing of sociological, pun. Everything considered, however, from one year and season to the next, the difference between a bar and no-bar river on the north shore today seems to have become mainly a matter of degree.

The Heritage of Landscapes

EARLY ONE MORNING IN LATE JUNE, I ARRIVE AT Artist's Point, just north of the harbor in Grand Marais, to find a dense fog draped across the shore. The point's northern outcrops lie fully exposed to the onslaught of stiff winds and storm waves, and perhaps more than any other place on the Minnesota coast, they have come to symbolize the raw, expansive spirit of Lake Superior's landscape. In the late 1940s, the first of several art colonies was established at Grand Marais, and as the point's name suggests, the area's rugged natural beauty has attracted many artists, as well as scores of other visitors who come to make the rounds across the rocks, or simply to sit and look out at the oceanlike expanse of empty water. I return regularly to photograph the flow of light and weather, the passing of time and seasons, across the dark, angular rock walls. This morning, however, the landscape looks as shapeless and indistinct as if viewed through frosted glass. The fog has thrown a wrench in my plans, and I have little choice but to leave my camera in the car.

Many of the rock walls at Artist's Point are straight enough to hang a plumb line snug against their faces. They bear the eroded marks of vertical joints that formed as the basaltic lavas cooled and contracted over a billion years ago. As the pounding of storm waves and freezing and thawing of winter waters expand the joints, small as well as boulder-size chunks of rock eventually fall away, leaving salmon-tinted cuts of unweathered basalt on the walls' lichen-studded surfaces. I find it strange to think that time inflicts its ravages as inevitably on these walls as on my own skin. It is only the scale that is different, geologic versus human time. Fortunately, the latter is the scale that matters most to me, and measured against it, the rocks on Artist's Point are as solid and enduring as anything on earth, even if this morning they are little more than shadowy contours.

Like the Superior shoreline, the west coast of southern Sweden where I spent many summers as a child was raw and windswept, lined with small island havens for nesting birds. The area where our cottage lay was sandier and grassier and distinctly less rugged than the landscape of Artist's Point and many other places on the Minnesota and Ontario shores. The area's slender beaches and grass-clad dunes were also atypical of western Sweden, which fronts the Atlantic mainly with bare, glacially scoured granite. The sandy bays of Michigan and Wisconsin may best resemble our stretch of coastline. Yet, in general, similarities between the upper Midwest and southwestern Sweden are more apparent farther south and inland from the lake, where the descendants of Scandinavian immigrants still inhabit the forested groves and farmlands.

The two landscapes share many elements of a similar natural history, and it makes sense that they should have features in common. Both lie at the margins of the ancient cores of granitic rock around which the earth's continents took form. Both were ice-bound during the latest glacial period, and both mark the southern reaches of the vast boreal forests that encircle the Arctic tundra. But for all the similarities in appearance and terrain, I have not been back to the summer cottage since I was eighteen, and my recollections of the Swedish countryside are intuited and incomplete, infused with the kind of sentimental associations through which small twists of experience easily take on the status of livable truths.

What ties the two landscapes together for me is an instinctual and compelling affinity in feeling, a sense of familiarity that is unconsciously triggered when I pick up the scent of dry evergreen on a trail or see reindeer mosses, blueberries, and glacially deposited boulders in the forest. Perhaps more than anything else, the connection is triggered by the way I can feel the weather, slipping it on like a glove in the morning, by the brisk and breezy days that linger late into the Lake Superior summer and rarely relinquish their hold on the Swedish coast. The natural sensations of my childhood summers surface easily at Artist's Point, where the low-lying ledge catches the chill of lake air even on calm August days, and scattered clusters of harebells, familiar flowers of northern landscapes around the globe, dot the rock. There is also a small wind-stunted forest that rises from the point's center, where mosses, bunchberries, and blueberries cover thin, needle-strewn soils. This morning, drops of water hang like motionless tears from the needles of spruce and fir, suspended for minutes before they suck enough density from the air to fall to the ground.

Winding roads led through the rolling landscape around our cottage. The west coast back then was mostly farm country, wheat fields and cow pastures passed down the family lines, interspersed with small fishing villages. It was a place of hard work and generous decency, where people lived humble, honorable lives off the land and the sea—rarely saying more than a conversation demanded but still managing to reveal, through many simple acts of kindness, that they felt and thought much about the land and people around them.

West of the road, summer cottages took over from the farms, extending seaward to the thin forest of wind-stunted pines that bordered the beach. Most cottage owners lived in cities that lay within a two- or three-hour drive and spent their spring and fall weekends and summer vacations on the coast. My mother's cousin and her husband owned the cottage next to us, and a bare ten-minute walk away, my aunt and her family had their summer place. A nearby campground afforded the use of a pay phone and laundry machine, but for the most part, summer living was a no-frills experience. Like most cottages, ours had a simple layout, one larger room with two bedrooms barely large enough to turn around in and separated by curtains from the main living area. Like other people, we stored perishables in a root cellar under the kitchen floor, bathed in buckets of water drawn from the well, and used an outhouse.

The farm-rich areas around our cottage contributed their fair share to immigration and settlement in the upper Midwest. Swedish emigration took off in the late 1860s. Early emigrant flows were dominated by farm families fleeing crop failures and land pressures brought on by rapid population growth. With much of the eastern United States already settled, immigrants moved into the upper Midwest in search of farmland. The first director of the Minnesota immigration board, which was established in 1867, was a Swede by the name of Hans Mattson. One of the relatively few Swedes who had arrived before the Civil War, Mattson was the son of a fairly prosperous farmer from the southern province of Skåne, and in 1853 had founded the "Mattson settlement," now the town of Vasa in southeastern Minnesota.

The immigration board disseminated information to potential immigrants on farmland, homesteading, and work opportunities in Minnesota through newspaper articles and pamphlets, many of which were written by Mattson, and published in various languages, including Swedish, Norwegian, and Danish. As elsewhere in the country, settlement was closely tied to the extension of railroads. Railroads not only transported immigrants but having received sizable government land grants along their proposed routes, sold land to prospective settlers, whose new farms and towns expanded the demand for train service. Subsidiary associations logged the land for track ties and timber profits, and then

parceled it out and attracted settlers by distributing promotional
materials through networks of local and overseas agents. They
worked closely with the state immigration board, coordinated
with steamship operators to transport emigrants from their native countries to specific destinations, and established Reception
Houses where immigrants could live for free until they were able
to locate suitable farmland.

Between, and sometimes alongside, his work as immigration
director and Minnesota secretary of state, Mattson served as a land
agent for both the Northern Pacific and the St. Paul and Mississippi
railroad companies; the former was financed largely by Jay Cooke
and eventually assumed the latter. Eager to promote rapid settlement in the area, Cooke set up land and emigration departments
for the Northern Pacific and convinced Mattson to return to
Sweden in the early and mid-1870s to encourage emigrants headed
for America to come to Minnesota. As Mattson mentions in his
1892 book *Reminiscences,* he received twice the amount of his state
salary from Cooke; he also profited by starting a banking and cur-
rency exchange firm, Mattson & Co., that among its other operations, sold pre-paid steamship tickets to immigrants.

In one of the many promotional pamphlets he authored,
Mattson writes glowingly of the similarities between the natural
features and "sound and wholesome" climates of Minnesota and
southern Sweden. The brochure mentions Minnesota's "picturesque" lake country and introduces Lake Superior as the world's
largest inland sea, and Duluth as a future port site contingent
only on the completion of the railroad north from Saint Paul.
The brochure goes on to describe the rich farm and pasture land
for sale between Saint Paul and Duluth, emphasizing the area's
rock-free soils, no doubt an added attraction for Swedish farm-
ers used to laboriously clearing their land and lining their fields
with long stone walls. Noting that "nature wastes its richest gifts"
in the region, Mattson details harvest amounts for wheat, corn,
potato, sorghum, beans, and other crops. He also presents work
opportunities in logging and railroad construction and in towns

along the tracks, which many immigrants relied on to either build up capital for their farms or, if poorer, to save enough to purchase land. By the late 1880s, with most of the state's good land settled and more young, single men leaving Scandinavia, nonfarm employment became even more important to attracting immigrants.

If Mattson believed that Minnesota was the "most suitable place" for Scandinavians to settle in America, he was not the first Swede to have experienced a sense of familiarity upon seeing the state. The Swedish socialite and novelist Fredrika Bremer had felt the same during her visit to the Saint Paul area in 1850. In her book *The Homes of the New World: Impressions of America,* Bremer too commented on how much Minnesota's rich soils, rivers, valleys, lakes, and "healthy, invigorating climate" reminded her of Sweden. So compelling did the affinity strike her that she made her now famous prediction, "what a glorious new Scandinavia might not Minnesota become!"

Our summer days on the Swedish west coast followed a fairly predictable routine. We played on the field and went to the beach, where we spent most of our time paddling around in a small wooden boat, lying in the lee of a dune or pine grove, and braving the cold, seaweed-laden waters. Occasionally, we got up at five and rode on the back of the tractor to watch the farmer up the road milk his cows. We also saw pigs come into the world in his barn, and one summer we borrowed a calf, whom we called Sylvia in honor of the Swedish queen, and staked her on our field. As obedient as a well-trained dog, she allowed herself to be led by her big, dangling metal chain along the back roads to the beach and campground. Unfortunately, she bellowed loudly in nightly communications with her siblings up the road and soon had to be returned. For a while, we tried a goat.

Some days, we rode our bicycles to the nearby village to buy fresh fish or went into Falkenberg, a small city a fifteen-minute drive to the south, to shop and take hot showers. Like many other Swedish cities, Falkenberg has medieval roots, with an old town quarter lined with quaint wooden houses and shops and cobble

streets. A few evenings each summer, we also accompanied our relatives into Varberg, a larger port city to the north, to go for coffee at
the terrace café of the main attraction, a thirteenth-century moated
fortress overlooking the sea. The fortress's museum is world-
renowned for the peat-preserved body and clothing of a man who
was murdered and thrown into a bog six hundred years ago.

Some of my fondest memories of our west coast summers
are of the frequent evening coffee gatherings with relatives and
neighbors, or whoever else happened to drop in on the cottage.
Drinking coffee is a deeply ingrained social ritual among my parents' generation of Swedes, and in the countryside people often
arrived unexpectedly. Many cottages, including ours, did not
initially have a phone, but arriving unannounced was also a way
of ensuring that one's hosts did not go to the trouble of any advance preparations. Impromptu visits were not confined to those
who lived nearby since with most businesses closed down, people
could usually be counted on to be at their cottages during the
month-long summer vacation. If they happened not to be home,
chances were good that they had gone for a swim or to get groceri-
ies and would soon be back. If after an hour or two, they had not
returned, one simply left a note and started for home, with little
more to show for the day's outing than some hundred-odd scenic
miles and a picnic.

Wherever we visited or whoever stopped in, the coffee ritual
proceeded in a similar fashion. Danish or pastry was served first,
followed by an assortment of cookies and then a cake. Almost
everything was homemade, having been prepared beforehand
and stored in the freezer or root cellar in anticipation of the not
so unexpected occasional appearance of surprise guests. Etiquette
required that guests not sample anything until invited to do so by
the hostess and that they proceed with polite restraint. An hour
or so after the cake had been cleared, fruits, sodas, and chocolates
were brought out. A short while later, guests usually began to
check their watches and comment on the time. Replete with its
own ritual, the process of leave-taking could easily add another

hour to the visit as guests acceded to one or more entreaties to
stay longer.

The coffee gatherings were, along with holiday and birthday
celebrations, among the few times I remember when stories and
laughter and ties of friendship and family seemed to flow freely
within my parents' circle. Many late evenings when guests were
at our cottage, my sister and I would lie awake in our bunk beds,
trying hard not to fall asleep, listening to the reassuring banter of
grown-ups through the curtain. I have long since realized that the
same adults who played and joked with us children also worked
hard and worried, and that when at their summer places, they
spent much of their time on the labor their old wooden cottages
and sandy, pine-studded yards required.

I have heard that the countryside around our cottage has
changed in the two decades since I last saw it. The area today is a
popular vacation destination, a Swedish Riviera as guidebooks call
it. Rows of modern homes line the old wheat fields and pastures.
The small fishing village where we used to buy the day's catch
fresh off the dock now caters to the tourist and yacht crowd, and
lined with long sandy beaches, the city to the south does a thriv-
ing resort business. The coast, inevitably, has lost its innocence.
In a way, it had begun to do so even before my last visit, when the
first fields started to be sold off and old-timers, such as my parents
and relatives, winterized and remodeled, adding indoor baths,
modern kitchens, and private bedrooms to their once simple cottages. The gravel road that led past our house, on which the soles
of my feet became thickly calloused, had been paved, and one or
two of the people I remember best had already passed on.

Yet if the place was changing, so was I. By the time I reached
my teens, I had begun to grow out of what the cottage had to
offer. The coast ceased to be a place of childhood fun and freedom and became instead a stifling reminder of the family ties that
I fought hard to break. And then there was the memory of my
cat, the runt without a sense of smell that I had trained to walk
leashless next to me like a dog. She was born into a litter of strays.

I had taken her in when she was only two weeks old, and I absolutely adored her. One day, I lost sight of her in a small forest near the cottage. Knowing the fate that would surely befall a cat unable to smell danger lurking, I looked for her every day until late summer, when we moved back to the city. Haunted by images of her helplessness, I spent the winter convinced that she was alive and snug in a barn and would be waiting for me on the stoop come spring. Cats that I had raised had died before, but not knowing the fate of something you love is so much worse. The hope that was inevitably dashed each time I arrived at the cottage stuck to the place. Soon I felt as if I were going there mainly to wager on the small chance that she would reappear, only to be disappointed every time.

As my recollections of our summers on the Swedish coast grow more distant with the years, I think I am gradually beginning to understand the time warp on which the nostalgia of older immigrants feeds—that of people who either came to this country as children or were born here and grew up listening to their parents' stories of the old country. Like me, many have little real contact with the places they trace themselves to, and the world they envision or may have distant memories of is far removed from the changes that passing time has brought to the Swedish countryside.

Faint rays of sunshine have begun to slowly work their way through the fog. If I am lucky, in half an hour or so, it may be clear enough for me to get out my camera. Yet the impatience I felt before has largely vanished. In its place, the familiar flow of landscapes has left a comfortable sense of arrested time. It is reassuring to know how effortlessly thoughts of passing seconds, minutes, and hours can give way, how easy it can be to unintentionally adjust to the pace of nature's clock. Perhaps this fog-induced waiver of time is what both I and the landscape needed, the outcrops receiving a respite from the waves, and I from a concept of time that is irrelevant to nature's scheme and, sometimes, to humans as well.

Harebells

THE SUPERIOR LANDSCAPE IS HARSH AND RUGGED, defined by a roughness that like the brush strokes in a van Gogh painting, creates an aesthetic of graceful unrefinement by refusing to embellish for embellishment's sake. Vast stretches of rocky coastline make for a difficult growing environment, and on the storm-etched ledges of the Minnesota shore, life is lean and functional. Few flowers can survive the fierce winds and cold sprays that press down against the rock, brushing before them the minute eroded particles out of which soils are born, and bringing injury or death to anything that is not hardy and firmly planted. Of those that can survive, the harebells are the most conspicuous. Well adapted to hardship and exposure, their delicate blue clusters are common on windswept northern meadows, mountains, and coastlines. More than any other flower, they are emblems of northern summer for me.

Superior's cold, oceanlike waters chill the air and delay the coming of summer to the coastal rock. The first flowers usually do not appear until sometime in mid-June, when three-toothed

cinquefoils gradually emerge from soil-filled crevices, and butterworts start to cling to the damp walls of shallow rock pools. Farther
up the shore, where the soils are deeper and shrubs and grasses
provide a minimum of shelter from the wind, wild strawberries,
dandelions, and the occasional tall lungwort or nodding trillium
also appear. The harebells are rarely more than a week or two behind these early flowers, and by the time their bells begin to open,
the shore has usually taken on a cheerful but muted look, dappled
in a progression of widely scattered colors.

Harebells may not be the first to appear, but they grace the rock
almost all summer long, from late June well into September. They
are most abundant from mid-July to mid-August, but more than a
few straggling bells can always be found swaying in the breeze with
the goldenrods, tansies, hawkweeds, asters, and other fall flowers.
Harebells are also rather prolific bloomers, with each rootstock giving rise to anywhere from one to several stems, and each stem carrying as many as six bells. The color of individual bells, including
in the same cluster, can vary widely from a deep, saturated violet
to a pale, almost satin lavender or heavenly blue. The longer a bell
hangs on, the paler and more translucent it becomes, until finally,
well into the process of drying out and shriveling up, it assumes
the shade and texture of old-fashioned silk paper. Most clusters
contain bells in various stages of bloom, and chances are good that
as one bell withers, another is opening up. Where summers are
short, it is hard not to place a premium on flowers that provide
such generous doses of color all season long.

Harebells excel at finding microhabitats to suit their growing conditions, and by clinging to fissures in the rock, they can
make do with bare threads of soil almost invisible to the eye. Their
tolerance for sandy, gravelly, and otherwise arid and nutrient-poor
soils has enabled them to thrive in a vast range of environments.
Yet they still need enough soil in which to secure their roots, and
while rocky coastal outcrops may support scattered clusters, large
colonies are most common on grassy fields and upland meadows.
Key to the harebell's versatility is its ability to withstand the force

and desiccation of the strong winds that sweep across the open landscapes it inhabits. To say that appearances can be deceiving is to state the obvious when it comes to the harebell. The plant's hairlike stems, while fragile-looking, are strong and supple, and for all their bobbing about, the bells themselves are securely attached.

Bell-shaped flowers, moreover, may have a reproductive advantage in exposed environments since the drooping bells protect the flower's nectar and pollen from rain and wind. Yet because the nectaries are well hidden inside the bells, the range of possible pollinators is limited to long-tongued insects and birds. On the Superior shore, this means mainly the bumblebee. Not surprisingly, the large bee has a difficult time getting at the harebell's nectar, and as it struggles, its pollen-laden body is all but guaranteed to brush against the flower's stigma, thus ensuring that fertilization takes place.

Most of us probably have a favorite flower, our preferences shaped by our liking for certain colors, textures, shapes, and sizes, as well as by the memories and experiences we associate with the places where such a flower is commonly found. I have a special affection for harebells. They are well suited to the northern environments that I like best, and I admire the tenacity and resilience that life in such places requires. Yet my affection also stems from a more personal source. Harebells grew in abundance on the small field that bordered my family's summer cottage on the Swedish coast. They remind me of the easily had pleasures of childhood and of a raw but generous landscape of farms, forests, and fields in the days before the area became a popular vacation destination.

My sister and I thought that the field was part of my family's summer property, but it actually belonged to our uncle, and one day it was sold. Before long, a new house went up—a house that while wood-clad and modest, had no history of belonging, so unlike the well-worn farmhouses where my grandparents had rented rooms when they first began visiting the coast, or the small cottages that they and other early summer residents later built. Our field was neither the first nor the last of the surrounding countryside to be sold. Where harebells and grasses used to sway, neat rows of vacation homes took hold, looking as out of place to me as the suburban boxes that sprout like weeds from the naked ground of old midwestern cornfields. With the homes soon came the paved roads and indoor plumbing that made life easier and more comfortable but that robbed the landscape of much of its old-country charm.

Harebells are common throughout Sweden, and our field held but a small piece of this northern treasure. I think it is only fitting that the flower should first have been described, in 1753, by the famous Swedish botanist and father of modern plant taxonomy Carl von Linné, or Linnaeus. Linnaeus must have seen many harebells in his day, and as a devout man, the flower's religious symbolism, of peace, piety, and the heavens, was probably not lost on him. More important for the future of science, Linnaeus believed that God had created a well-ordered world, and in the hopes of uncovering the divinely ordained nature of things, he spent much of his life organizing and classifying plants. In the process, he laid the foundations for modern scientific taxonomy and botanical nomenclature.

The inventory of natural species was expanding rapidly in Linnaeus's day as European explorers and travelers in the New World brought back reports and specimens of previously un-known plants and animals. Linnaeus's interest in plant classifica-tion, and the religious conviction that lay behind it, was hardly exceptional among eighteenth-century botanists, who in response to the growing number of known species, had become increasing-ly eager for a logical classificatory scheme. A fundamental ques-tion remained unresolved, however, namely, what criteria to use when attempting to group and determine relationships among plants. As Aristotle had initially recognized, the use of different criteria often produced incompatible classifications for the same natural objects. The sixteenth-century Flemish botanist Matthias de L'Obel had proposed classifying plants according to leaf shape, whereas the late-seventeenth-century Frenchman Joseph Pitton de

Tournefort favored flower form. Plants grouped as closely related based on one similarity could end up having little or nothing in common if classified according to another.

While various criteria had previously been proposed, in Linnaeus's time much of botanical research was devoted to the study of sexuality in plants. In 1737, in a work called *Genera Plantarum*, Linnaeus accordingly introduced a system for grouping plants based on the number and arrangement of their male and female reproductive organs. The Sexual System, as he called it, quickly established Linnaeus as one of Europe's leading scientists. Above all else, the system had the advantage of simplicity, requiring little more than a count of male, pollen-producing stamens, according to which plants were divided into one of twenty-four classes, and of female pistils, which as a subordinate criterion, provided a basis for breaking the classes into smaller orders. Linnaeus described his system by comparing stamens and pistils to grooms and brides, or to husbands and wives, who depending on the arrangement of floral reproductive parts, could be thought of as sleeping in the same or different beds, or as engaging in lawful or unlawful sexual relations.

The system was not without its critics, including those who opposed Linnaeus's explicit use of human analogies. More important, as even Linnaeus recognized, classifying plants according to elements of appearance, such as the number of reproductive parts, produced seemingly artificial groupings that incorporated large numbers of species with little in common save for the number of their stamens. By the late 1700s, botanists increasingly turned to a more "natural system" for classification that was rooted in actual evolutionary relationships among plants. Building on the work of the English naturalist John Ray, in 1789 the French botanist Antoine-Laurent de Jussieu accordingly proposed using multiple characteristics to group flowering plants into monocots and dicots, depending on whether they had one or two seed leaves, and to subsequently subdivide them into classes, which were in turn broken into families. In the Lake Superior region, examples of monocots, which often have flower parts in multiples of three and display striking, showy blossoms, can be found among the Iris, Lily, and Orchid families, and of the dicots, whose flower parts tend to come in multiples of four or five, among the Geranium, Crowfoot, Heath, Gentian, and Bluebell families.

As far as taxonomy is concerned, pre-Linnaean botanists labored under the assumption that it was necessary to first assign plants to large, inclusive groups based on very generally shared characteristics, and only thereafter subdivide them into progressively smaller units whose members possessed more specific commonalities. Linnaeus reversed this order. To accurately depict the varied relationships among different organisms, he concluded, scientific classification had to take as its starting point not the largest but the smallest category, the individual species, whose members were more closely related to one another than to those of any other species. From this most basic unit, modern plant taxonomy works up the hierarchy by combining plants into progressively more inclusive groupings of genus, family, order, class, and phylum, with the degree of their relatedness diminishing at each level.

Linnaeus's main contribution lay in devising a universal system of scientific nomenclature. A plant's name, he believed, should describe one or more of its distinguishing features, such as its preferred habitat or the shape of its flowers or leaves, and identify the closest group of related species to which it belongs. Previous botanists had come up with various approaches for referring to plants, many of which relied on descriptive Latin phrases or cumbersome sentences that often varied from one user to the next. Linnaeus saw the need for a universal nomenclature, and in the 1753 edition of his book *Species Plantarum,* he introduced a method for referring to plants through the use of two names, a genus name followed by a one-word species-specific indicator, both italicized and given in Latin or having been Latinized.

The harebell's scientific name, thus, is *Campanula rotundifolia,* round-leafed bell. The genus name *Campanula,* which comes from the Latin word for "bell," indicates that the plant belongs to a larger grouping of bell-shaped flowers, while the species adjective *rotundifolia* is a descriptor for the round leaves that appear briefly at the base of a harebell's stem before it comes into bloom. As set forth under the Linnaean system, a plant's genus name may sometimes honor a fellow botanist who may or may not also have discovered it. Linnaeus's favorite flower was the trailing pink "twinflower," which is common to northern evergreen forests. Its scientific name, *Linnea borealis,* both honors Linnaeus and denotes its preferred boreal forest habitat.

The idea of a two-name system had initially been suggested by the French botanist Charles de L'Ecluse in 1576, and again by the Swiss botanist and physician Caspar Bauhin in 1623. In the last decades of the seventeenth century, Ray had described the concept of species, and Tournefort that of genus. It fell to Linnaeus, however, to systematically develop a unified system of binomial nomenclature that could identify the taxonomical relationships among species and be applied to all natural objects. To this end, he tried to personally name and describe every known plant, mineral, and animal, including *Homo sapiens.*

The existence of a universal scientific nomenclature is fortunate, for unlike common or popular names, the Linnaean system enables scientists from every corner of the world to use a uniform vocabulary for identifying species. Common names frequently differ from place to place; moreover, identical common names are sometimes used to refer to unrelated species. The harebell, for instance, is popularly called a bluebell. Yet it is also known by other names, such as lady's thimble, and on the Superior shore it is not the only flower that is sometimes referred to as a bluebell.

The name "tall bluebell" is used locally to refer to *Mertensia paniculata,* or tall lungwort, a more northerly and westerly relation of the better-known Virginia bluebell. A much larger and shrubbier plant, the tall bluebell grows in moist soils at the edge of the forest along the shore. Like the harebell, it has blue, bell-shaped flowers, its clusters of small buds turning from a pearly lavender to a beautiful coral blue as they open. Despite what their similar common names may suggest, however, the two flowers are completely unrelated. One belongs to the *Mertensia* genus, named after the German botanist Franz Karl Mertens, and to the larger Boraginaceae, or Forget-me-not family, the other to the "bell" genus and the Campanulaceae, or Bluebell family.

In Linnaeus's day, Latin was still commonly taught in the schools, and most educated people would have been able to understand the meaning of a plant's scientific name. This is no longer the case, and modern botany has had to make some concessions in the interest of giving nonscientists some hope of learning to identify plants. My National Audubon Society field guide, which was originally published in 1979, is divided into two sections. The first, the color plates, organizes flowers into eight color groups, the larger of which are further broken down according to form, simple- or odd-shaped flowers, rounded or elongated clusters, and so forth. Once a likely identification has been made based on such considerations, information on flower structure, habitat, and range can be found by turning to the family and species descriptions. Unlike the plates, the descriptions are scientifically organized.

If color plates make for easy identification, they are of little help in understanding relationships among the various species. This much is evident from a quick glance at the section on blue odd-shaped flowers, in which the harebell can be found. The ten flowers that appear in the section represent seven different families—Bluebell, Buttercup, Gentian, Iris, Mint, Snapdragon, and Spiderwort—and most have nothing in common except for their color and unusual shape. Moreover, in the 2001 Audubon field guide, the harebell is classified not as an odd-shaped flower, a designation that has been eliminated from the updated version, but as a blue, radially symmetrical flower.

My bookshelf includes the occasional scientific field guide, yet I do not plan to wean myself from more popularly accessible works anytime soon. Color plates hold too many advantages for me. Not the least of these is that in a frequently referenced guide, the order of the plates and often the placement and appearance of the flowers on a page become second nature. I may never have identified a particular species before, but I will have seen its photograph countless times while searching my guidebook for other flowers. If I eventually encounter it in the field, I can usually visualize its approximate location among the color plates, and if lucky, sometimes even recall the name that appears under its photograph.

There is a final and obvious benefit to be gained from color plates. Unlike the actual flowers they depict, they never fade. This may seem trivial, but in northern landscapes, I hardly think it is. There have been times when during the dreariest part of winter, I have pulled the Audubon from its shelf and leafed my way through hundreds of glossy close ups of flowers in the height of bloom. The harebell appears near the end of the color plates, sharing a well-worn page with the fringed gentian, the crested dwarf iris, and the blue flag. Like a treasured keepsake, its pale, rain-soaked bells remind me that as surely as the earth continues to rotate around the sun, the colors of summer will soon return to Lake Superior's shore.

The Group of Seven at Coldwell

IN THE FALL OF 1921, CANADIAN ARTIST LAWREN Harris visited Neys Provincial Park on the Coldwell Peninsula for the first time. Drawn to northern regions, Harris was fascinated with the colossal shapes formed by the rocks and clouds, and the austere flow of light across the Superior landscape. Painting for him was part of a spiritual quest, and on Lake Superior's northern shore, he found a landscape sufficiently stark, barren, and expansive to give artistic expression to his beliefs. Accompanied by other artists from the Group of Seven, he painted from Heron Bay west to Rossport between 1923 and 1928, returning to the Coldwell Peninsula several times. In one of his most famous works, he used a few simple forms and contrasting colors to render Pic Island off the coastline of Neys. The canvas epitomizes the bold, abstract style through which the Group of Seven charted a novel course in modern Canadian art, with Harris as its key organizer.

Pic Island and a few of Harris's other north shore works hang in a small corner of the Neys visitor center. Accompanying text provides a brief overview of Harris's life and visits to the Coldwell area. The artist, I read, apparently often used the fishing village of Coldwell, on the peninsula's southeastern tip, as a base from which to explore Neys and the surrounding coastline. Following a cairned trail at Neys, I can easily see why Harris was inspired by the Coldwell region and why the rare syenitic rock forms he encountered there had such a profound influence on his artistic style.

What is less easy to understand is why the unique natural history of this gem of a park was not featured more prominently in many of the guidebooks I had read. The rock-born story of the Coldwell Peninsula seems to be easily overshadowed by unsolved mysteries and unsavory tidbits of human history. The peninsula's cobble beaches contain stone structures believed to have been built by native Ojibwe over two thousand years ago. To date, more than three hundred Pukaskwa Pits have been found on the Canadian shore, yet their function, whether sacred or practical, has largely remained a mystery. Telescope history and the present campground of Neys Provincial Park was the site of one of Canada's nine "black" POW camps, which were set up during World War II to accommodate potentially dangerous high-ranking German officers, who, isolated by the vast waters and forested wilderness, would be unlikely to survive an attempted escape. The Neys park brochure includes an old photograph of the former barracks and barbed wire fencing, no evidence of which remains today. Fortunately, it also includes a photograph of Harris's painting of Pic Island. Had I not chanced on a copy of the brochure and seen the *Pic Island* photograph while visiting nearby Pukaskwa National Park, I would have passed Neys by.

The Group of Seven was a loose collection of Toronto-based artists that took its name from the original seven painters who exhibited their work together at the city's Art Gallery in 1920. Harris provided much of the artistic vision that lay behind the Group's popular success. Central to this vision was a belief that in both style and substance Canadian landscape painting needed to be detached from its European, and especially English, roots. Having studied and traveled in Europe, Harris and other Group members had been strongly influenced by the plein air approach of the French impressionists. Yet they saw the imitative bucolic style common among Canadian turn-of-the-century painters as unsuited to capturing the wild and expansive character of their country's landscape. They wanted, as Harris later wrote in *The Story of the Group of Seven,* to paint in a way that would "embody the moods and character and spirit of the country."

Harris's ideas on what a national art form might look like had begun to take shape a few years before World War I, when he met several artists who shared his longing for an authentic Canadian style of painting, including J. E. H. MacDonald, A. Y. Jackson, and Tom Thomson. By the time the Group of Seven was formally established in 1920, Harris and several of its other members had been painting together, usually traveling in groups of two to four, for a decade. Starting out in and around Toronto, they gradually began to paint farther afield, using weekends and summer vacations to travel to Algonquin Provincial Park, Algoma, the Georgian Bay, and Lake Superior and eventually also to the Rockies, the Arctic, and other northern regions. Their movement beyond Toronto and into Canada's northern landscape reflected a growing conviction that it was in nature, not in the urban, industrial society unfolding before them, that the essence of their country's spirit lay.

For Harris, this conviction had been reinforced by a 1913 New York exhibit of contemporary Scandinavian painting in Buffalo. The exhibit, which Harris attended with MacDonald, had a defining impact on the future direction of the Group of Seven's work. "Here was a landscape as seen through the eyes [and] felt through the hearts . . . of people who knew and loved it," Harris later observed; "an art, bold, vigorous, and uncompromising, embodying direct experience of the great North. . . . From that time on we knew that we were at the beginning of an all-engrossing adventure." The adventure on which Harris and other Group members embarked ultimately led to the development of a unique artistic style that was rooted in a distinct subject matter, the landscape of the Canadian north and especially of northern Ontario, as well as to a distinct compositional technique, the use of large, simple forms and bold, contrasting colors.

World War I temporarily scattered the artists, but the end of the war brought a heightened sense of urgency to their search for an independent Canadian style of painting. In 1918, they began to paint together again, and during the summer, Harris had a railway boxcar outfitted for use as a studio and residence while they explored the Algoma region east of Lake Superior. Not all Group artists were equally enthusiastic outdoorsmen, but depending on financial circumstances and other obligations, they tried to spend anywhere from several weeks to months each year in the field, sketching and making oil studies for canvases that were later worked up in their Toronto studios. Most supported themselves as commercial or graphic artists. Harris alone came from a socially prominent family and as heir to a large fortune, was able to pursue his artistic vision unencumbered by everyday financial obligations. His vision included encouraging a continuous flow of ideas, inspiration, and support among artists who shared his quest for a more authentic style of Canadian painting. In 1913, he financed most of the construction of the three-story Toronto Studio Building, in which several future Group artists found affordable studios as well as living and gathering space.

With some variations in membership, the Group of Seven remained together until 1931, when it held its final exhibit. Its innovative style, the antithesis of the calm, polished work of mainstream Canadian painters, quickly became highly controversial within the Toronto-based art establishment. Yet its annual exhibits were popular with the public, and as self-described rebels, the reputation of artistic radicals suited the artists well.

Harris's approach to the Canadian landscape drew inspiration from the transcendentalist ideas of Ralph Waldo Emerson, Henry David Thoreau, and other nineteenth- and early-twentieth-century American literary figures. Thoreau's statement in his 1862 essay "Walking," "I must walk toward Oregon, and not toward

Europe," reflected the basic transcendentalist goal of breaking with European conventions and developing a new literature rooted in the particulars of the American landscape and experience. Emerson, whose 1836 *Nature* had provided the impetus for the emergence of the transcendentalist movement, believed that through intuition and direct experience with the natural world, humans could transcend their physical existence and reach a state of unison with the divine "spark," or Oversoul. Natural forms, he believed, were symbols of spiritual meaning, and if read correctly, they could provide humans with enlightenment and insight. Harris saw his country's spirit reflected most fully in wild and expansive northern regions and found the vast waters and simple rocks of the Superior shore ideal for conveying this yearning for spiritual revelation through nature. The mysticism and quest for spiritual understanding that inspired canvases such as *Pic Island, Lake Superior, Sketch II,* and *From the North Shore* had also found expression in a 1922 collection of poems, *Contrasts*.

As Harris returned to Neys and surrounding areas, he began to paint with greater symbolism and sparsity of form and color. Striving to reveal the underlying essence of a scene, he increasingly reduced the landscape to what he saw as its most elemental features, the flow of light and the arrangement of shapes and shadows. Many of his north shore canvases consist of a few prominent forms—clouds, islands, or stretches of coastline, each rendered in bold, contrasting shades of a single color, blue, brown, white, or yellow—and the pronounced flow of light across the water. Painting on the north shore and in the Canadian Rockies and the Arctic during the last half of the 1920s, he moved farther and farther along the path of abstraction. In so doing, he added impetus to artistic ideas that had been evolving for over a decade among Group of Seven artists, many of whom accompanied him to Coldwell. After the Group held its final exhibit in 1931, Harris gave up landscape painting altogether and devoted the rest of his career to abstract art. Yet it was in the depiction of the Canadian landscape that his artistic legacy lay.

Few other places around Lake Superior afford a better lesson in rock-born abstraction than does the coastline of Neys Provincial Park. Gently rolling, elongated syenite humps and ridges extend like whale backs along the water's edge, creating the smooth, bare, and simple kind of scenery to which Harris was attracted. Syenite is a relatively rare rock, and around the lake, it crops up only on the Coldwell Peninsula. Like granite, to which it is related, minus most or all of the quartz granite contains, syenite is an igneous rock and is often found as smaller intrusions, such as dikes and sills, in older bedrock and especially at the edges of larger bodies of granite. The syenite at Neys is part of the Coldwell Alkaline Complex, the largest concentration of alkaline rocks in North America, and was laid down during a sequence of three volcanic eruptions during the midcontinental rift upheavals 1.1 billion years ago.

The Under the Volcano Trail, which follows a short stretch of coastline at Neys, leads into the center of what was once the volcano's giant magma chamber. The volcano itself and the two kilometers of rock that originally separated its chamber from the earth's surface above have eroded away, exposing the syenite outcrops across which the trail leads. A definite highlight of the trail is a series of placards describing noteworthy geological phenomena underfoot. Unlike the cursory observations commonly encountered on park trails, the placards at Neys furnish detailed yet accessible information and are refreshing in their assumption that I and other park visitors, while in all likelihood novices to geology, can nevertheless benefit from detailed explanations of the phenomena we observe.

After each eruption, as one placard explains, the volcano's empty magma chamber collapsed and filled anew, causing each of the three eruptions to have a slightly different mineral composition. As a result, the Coldwell Peninsula consists of three distinct types of syenite: augite-amphibole syenite, which is close to black and dominates the eastern region; ferro-edenite, which has a pinkish cast and forms a small area on the northwestern edge of the Coldwell Complex; and nepheline, the rarest of the three, which tends toward a greasy whitish gray and crops up between the other two syenites, including at Neys.

A strong and resistant rock, syenite takes its name from the early Egyptian city of Syene, today Aswân, on the east bank of the Nile. The ancient Egyptians quarried a rock that was later called syenite, but was actually a pink granite, for use in embellishing pyramids, monuments, and obelisks during the reign of the pharaohs. Syenite continues to have commercial applications, including as a building material, and nepheline rock, which has a very pale and sometimes even whitish shade, is especially valued in the making of porcelain.

In painting Pic Island and other north shore places, Harris favored smooth contours and nonrepresentational forms. The finer details of the coastal rock, while not ignored, were rendered sparingly and selectively. Yet the syenite at Neys is as interesting for its small details as it is for its bold forms. Small prisms and patches of pink, red, and black minerals, their various compositions explained by the placards, form endless interesting streaks and patterns, and delicate light pink lines extend like interlocking webs across the smooth black surfaces of scattered boulders. In some areas, the contrast in colors is on a much grander scale. Large, dark gray swirls wind their way through sections of pink-tinted rock, and elsewhere large bands of assorted shades and textures combine to form a vast canvas of abstract patterns. The bands represent distinct mineral layers that formed along the magma chamber's cooler base and walls. Earthquakes and tremors caused the layers to fall into the chamber's fluid center, where turbid currents worked them like giant ladles, stirring and haphazardly juxtaposing them against layers with different mineral compositions and grain sizes.

For all the rock's interesting details, I think Harris was basically right. The abstract forms of ridges and outcrops and the smooth undulating shadows through which their contours emerge are what catch the eye on the coastline at Neys. Harris did not approach Lake Superior as a place to be rendered accurately on a canvas. He searched its rocks for simple, compelling forms through which nature's transcendent spirit could be revealed. He exalted a rich body of human sentiment in rendering the Coldwell coast, adding his vision to a prodigious collection of poems, paintings, and stories—a few of equal, but many of less, renown—that draw their inspiration from the landscape of the lake.

I am at the tail end of my trip, planning to drive west toward Thunder Bay and back into Minnesota tomorrow. What I see at Neys comes as an unexpected surprise, final icing on a cake I thought I had already sampled the best of. Guidebooks may accord it relatively scant attention, yet the coastline at Neys forms as vital a part in the diversity of the Superior landscape as many of the places that I had carefully researched and incorporated into my itinerary. Looking down at the photograph of Harris's painting of Pic Island in the park brochure, I cannot help but wonder how many places like Neys I may have missed.

Louis Agassiz on the Eastern Shore

WITHOUT A DOUBT, CANADA HOLDS LAKE SUPERIOR'S wildest coastline. The longest protected coastal stretch, more than sixty miles of raw rock, lies in Lake Superior Provincial Park on the eastern Ontario shore. A thirty-three-mile trail, extending from Chalfant Cove south to Sinclair Cove, offers one of the few remaining places around the lake where it is possible to walk for hours, maybe even a day, and encounter no sign of humans' presence. The coastal rocks contain some of the oldest exposed land on earth, a geologic gold mine extending nearly 2.7 billion years back in time. As the famous Swiss geologist Louis Agassiz observed during his visit in 1848, they provide incontrovertible evidence of glaciation and ancient geologic upheaval. They also display the work of native rock artists who, several centuries ago, used their surfaces like giant canvases on which to render their dreams and legends. Fortunately, large swaths of the Canadian coast look much as they did in Agassiz's day, and the rocks still tell their story without interference.

Following the coastal trail north from Katherine Cove, the

long and tortuous history of the emergence of land on earth unfolds under my feet. The cliffs and outcrops are part of the Canadian Shield, a core of largely granitic rock around which the North American continent assembled. Like other shields, North America's consists largely of what are known as greenstone belts, folded, elongated bands of volcanic and sedimentary rocks that have been surrounded by large masses of granite and gneiss. The belts date to about 2.7 billion years ago, when the first slivers of land, early volcanic islands, began to break through the earth's watered surface after having gradually risen from the vast platform of ocean-floor basalt upon which they sat. Eventually, as the islands eroded, muds and sands settled in their offshore basins, and larger landmasses emerged.

The shallow, mineral-rich waters that surrounded these early lands gave rise to the earth's oldest known life forms, which consisted of thin mats of blue-green algae that spread across shallow, sunlit areas of the basin floors. As the mats piled up in layers, sediments became trapped between the algal threads, forming carpets of tightly spaced mounds on the sea floor. Eventually, the mounds were transformed into rock. Today, such "stony carpets," or stromatolites, contain the earth's oldest microfossils, some of which, in western Australia and southern Africa, have been dated at 3.5 billion years. In the early 1950s, they were discovered along the Schreiber channel on the Ontario shore, where they are 1.9 billion years old. They are also present in Minnesota's Mesabi Iron Range. We humans have a lot to thank for these ancient algal mats; in releasing oxygen as a by-product of photosynthesis, they began to create an atmosphere on earth that could sustain more complex life.

Like today's continents, early landmasses sat atop tectonic plates that moved in relation to one another like shifting pieces of a giant jigsaw puzzle. Where plates met and one slipped under the other, lands collided, were scraped off, and were folded into mountain ranges. Intense heat and pressure forced vast quantities of granitic magma toward the earth's surface, which both raised and metamorphosed the overlying rock. In the process, basalt was changed into greenstone, so named because of its chlorite-derived green tint, and the "greenstone belts" emerged as long islands amid great seas of granite. Eventually, these larger landmasses also collided, and subject to intense heat and pressure deep underground, granite was changed into gneiss.

Millennia of geologic upheaval and erosion have left stunning juxtapositions of shape, color, and texture in the Canadian coastal rock. Elsewhere around the lake, ledges and outcrops reveal their designs mainly to those who look closely. On the Canadian shore, however, nature's patterns have been writ in bold, eye-catching forms. Among the most spectacular of these forms are the dikes of dark gray and often vesicular basalt, and of smooth black diabase that cut dramatically through the light gray, white, and pink-tinted granite. The dikes' lava was laid down over a billion years ago, when midcontinental rift flows penetrated fractures in the older, granitic bedrock. Some of the dikes are massive and climb out of the water like giant staircases, having eroded along joint lines into irregular blocks that become progressively larger as they ascend from the lake. Others slice through the granite barely inches wide. In yet other places, strands of white quartz run like twine across the basalt's surface.

Following the coastal trail, I find myself thinking, not for the first time, how nice it would be to have a guidebook to Lake Superior's rocks, a photographic geology tour, replete with summary descriptions, of diabase dikes, granite cliffs, gneiss outcrops, and the like. I try to picture Louis Agassiz studying the coastal rocks, attempting to decipher how the system of dikes has shaped the Superior basin. Agassiz described the dike system and other features of the Canadian shore in a popular book called *Lake Superior,* which was published in 1850. A decade earlier, he had proposed his novel theory that glaciers had once covered large parts of the earth. The glacier, Agassiz believed, "was God's great plough," and it, not the giant flood or icebergs favored by many of his contemporaries, had scraped the land clean and left the scattered boulders and foreign debris that he had first observed while hiking in the Swiss Alps. Had glaciers not crossed the Superior basin, he suspected, none of the coast's ancient bedrock and dike system would be visible.

Agassiz spent the summer of 1848 traveling by canoe from Sault Sainte Marie to the Kaministiquia River north of Thunder Bay, hoping to prove that glacial action had not been not confined to Europe. To the naturalists and students who accompanied him, he was ceaselessly pointing out erratic boulders, glacially polished surfaces, and the terraces or former shorelines that glacial meltwaters had left high above the lake's present level. Although Agassiz never ventured west of the Kaministiquia, a vast postglacial lake that some 13,000 years ago spanned the present peatlands of southern Canada and the northern United States was named in his honor. Exceeding the collective surface area of the Great Lakes, Lake Agassiz emptied its early waters south through the Glacial River Warren, and around 9,000 years ago opened a temporary outlet into the Superior basin before shifting its drainage north toward Hudson Bay as the glaciers receded.

While later science proved Agassiz wrong on several counts, including his opposition to Darwinism and his belief that ice had once covered the entire earth, the signs of glaciation that he found can still be read clearly on Lake Superior's Canadian coast. In bringing his Ice Age theory across the Atlantic, he prompted American geologists to pay closer attention to the record of glaciation in North America, including around Lake Superior. Unfortunately, Agassiz made only one visit to Superior country. In 1847, he had accepted an appointment as chair in Natural History at Harvard University, and three years later, he gained a valuable life and work partner in his new wife, Elizabeth, who assisted him in recording field observations, preparing findings for publication, and writing several books, and also became the first president of Radcliffe College. Secure in work and family, Agassiz took to his adopted homeland with undisguised affection. He befriended Ralph Waldo Emerson, Henry David Thoreau, Oliver Wendell Holmes, and other prominent writers and thinkers and devoted the rest of his life to teaching and to building up Harvard's Museum of Comparative Zoology, which he had established and for which he had gathered rock samples as well as fish and plant specimens during his Lake Superior trip.

Moreover, Agassiz believed that natural history was part of people's heritage and that such knowledge should not be confined to the educated. He was determined to bring science to popular audiences, and while he moved in influential circles, he often eschewed the restrictive conventions of the New England elite. He traveled widely, speaking to packed lecture halls, his popularity aided by the budding scientific and educational awakening that emerged in the United States following the end of the Civil War and the publication of Darwin's *On the Origin of Species.* Amiable, engaging, and ever controversial, Agassiz became a giant in a field of less distinguished American players.

In an interesting twist, a little over two decades after Agassiz's travels around the lake, his son Alexander, a Harvard-educated civil engineer and scientist, became president of the consolidated Calumet and Hecla Mining Company, whose copper operations centered around a rich conglomerate lode in the middle of Michigan's Keweenaw Peninsula. Living on the peninsula in his early thirties, from the spring of 1867 to the fall of 1868, Alexander Agassiz turned the once failing company into a highly profitable venture that eventually provided him with a considerable personal fortune. He was known as a difficult and overbearing man but also as one who, in keeping with the corporate paternalism of his time, was deeply committed to the welfare of his workers and to building a strong community around his mine. He retained a nominal position as Calumet's president until his death in 1910 and continued to visit the Keweenaw twice a year. The younger Agassiz's real interests, however, lay in the scientific passions passed on from his father. He saw mining mainly as a means to obtaining the financial security with which to pursue his specimen collecting and oceanographic research, as well as to build up the Museum of Comparative Zoology, of which he became curator upon his father's death in 1873. He published several works, including the 1865 book *Seaside Studies in Natural History,* which he coauthored with his stepmother, Elizabeth.

During subsequent decades, Louis Agassiz's book on Lake Superior stimulated popular interest in the Canadian shore. Visitors began to trickle up from Sault Sainte Marie, joining loggers and prospectors who sought to carve a living out of the rocks and forests of the eastern shore. Evidence of old logging dams, mills, and mines can still be found along the coast, yet, fortunately, most of these structures were made out of wood and have long since burned down or rotted away.

Unfortunately, nature does not discriminate in what it reclaims, eroding the imprint of human history regardless of its merit, and the pictographs that native rock artists once left on Inscription Rock at Agawa Bay are vanishing as well. Most pictograph sites in the Superior region have been found in the Quetico-Superior wilderness; relatively few exist on the lake itself. The large granite wall called Inscription Rock in Lake Superior Provincial Park is a well-known site. Yet the wall sits only half a dozen feet or so from the water, and the symbols on its surface are gradually being eroded by the abrasive action of storm waves and shifting piles of winter ice. Canadian rock art researcher Selwyn Dewdney, who discovered hundreds of rock art sites on the Canadian Shield and coauthored *Indian Rock Paintings of the Great Lakes,* reported seeing sixty-odd symbols at Agawa Bay in 1958. Today, only thirty-five of these are still visible.

Rock art appears across the Canadian Shield. As elsewhere in North America, it was associated with the practice of shamanism. The rocks on which the figures and symbols appear were believed to contain resident spirits and to be sacred. They were places where shamans communicated with the spirit world and young men undertook vision quests. Like the words in a language, the canoes, animals, men, and other symbols that make up the Inscription Rock panel combine to tell a story. The story, as a park interpretive sign explains, is that of a war party that protected by the great underwater spirit, the horned Misshepezhieu, crossed safely from the southern to the northern lakeshore to help the Agawa Ojibwe in their fight against the Iroquois. As were other pictographs, the panel's renderings were finger-painted onto the rock with iron hematite, or red ochre, a mineral stain that was frequently used for sacred purposes throughout North America. Dewdney dated the site at no earlier than the mid-seventeenth century. Rock art, however, is part of an ancient tradition and may have entered areas south and west of the lake as early as the first Paleo-Indian migrations. The two-thousand-odd Jeffers petroglyphs in southwestern Minnesota date from five thousand years ago.

The accounts of early travelers around Lake Superior include several references to native rock art. Elliot Cabot's "Narrative of the Tour," which makes up the first part of Agassiz's *Lake Superior,* describes two sites on the northern shore, *Les Ecrits* and *Les Petits Ecrits.* At both, representations of canoes, caribou, snakes, and other figures were produced by scraping dark rock tripe, a common form of lichen, from the faces of granite walls. The physician John Bigsby, who accompanied a land survey team from Sault Sainte Marie to Grand Portage in 1823, mentioned the same two Written Rock sites in his 1850 book *The Shoe and Canoe.* A few years earlier, the explorer Joseph Nicollet had seen rock art along the Mississippi River. And petroglyphs, made by carving instead of painting the surface of the rock, had been reported on the limestone bluffs of the Mississippi by the missionary and explorer Jacques Marquette already in 1673.

The first serious attempt to describe Lake Superior's rock art was made by Henry Rowe Schoolcraft, who included renderings and descriptions of the Agawa Bay pictographs in his 1851 book on the American Indians. Schoolcraft, a geologist, ethnographer, and explorer, served as a federal Indian agent for the Michigan Territory's Sault Sainte Marie district, which included Lake Superior's northern Ojibwe population, and as Michigan Superintendent of Indian Affairs in the 1820s and 1830s. His marriage to the half-Ojibwe daughter of a prominent fur trader added to the intimate knowledge of native life, legend, and culture that he developed. While he never visited Agawa, Schoolcraft was fascinated by native myths and had been shown birch-bark scrolls of the Inscription Rock pictographs and been told the stories on which they were based by an Ojibwe chief. The 1851 book in which renderings of the pictographs appeared was but one of many significant publications by a man who is widely credited with being the first American scholar to attempt to provide a thorough and sensitive understanding of Native American beliefs and traditions.

Save for the red ochre figures, humans have left fewer traces of their presence on the Canadian coast than elsewhere around the lake. The coastal forest is largely post-logging regrowth, and scattered towns hug the highway between Sault Sainte Marie and Thunder Bay. Yet, Ontario's Lake Superior basin is sparsely populated, with 90 percent of its land in public hands, double the amount of the American side, much of it roadless. The waters are like an ocean, wild and expansive, and without the hint of an opposite shoreline. Following the coastal trail, I walk, as I rarely do in more heavily trampled landscapes, without ambivalence, relieved to have found a place that still displays a serene unawareness of human life. To my surprise, I easily shed my usual annoyance at happening on other people on the trail and even come to welcome the moments of camaraderie these chance encounters provide. The brief words exchanged and the assumption of shared sympathies with those one meets linger like a loose but comfortable blanket to be cast aside at will. Bearing fewer markers of the people who have crossed its surface, the ancient Canadian bedrock holds out hope that it may still be possible for us to tread gently and respectfully, to leave few signs of our intentions or desires, and to let the stories of the land continue to unfold without disturbance.

In the Shade of Pines

JUST WEST OF COPPER HARBOR, THE FORESTS OF THE
northern Keweenaw Peninsula rise from the shores of Lake
Superior and up the slopes of Brockway Mountain. A trail, across
the road from Esprey Park, leads into the heart of the Keweenaw
Shore and Lake Upson nature sanctuaries. The forest through
which it passes supports many common north woods trees. Yet
its signature species is the red pine. In the shade of its slender
crowns, some of the prettiest wildflowers of the northern forest
have come into bloom during the latter weeks of June.

The surprising variety of habitats produces a much richer
display of wildflowers than I am used to seeing in such a small
area of Superior woodlands. Yet, given annual variations in snowfall and in spring rain and temperatures around the lake, peak
flowering times are often difficult to get right. With a forecast of
continued cool weather and intermittent showers, I had planned
to spend my weekend on the Keweenaw exploring abandoned
copper mines, old native quarries, and other remnants of the
peninsula's rich human history. When I arrive at Copper Harbor,

however, the skies are clearing, and I decide to scrap my original plans in favor of visiting a few of the area's natural sanctuaries. Riding the tide of unforeseen opportunities is often a must when exploring the Superior region.

Several natural environments are close together on the Keweenaw's northern tip, and deciding which to visit is not easy. Among the best known is the Estivant Pines Wilderness Sanctuary, a lowland of old-growth white pines whose moist and densely shaded soils provide an ideal habitat for many species of orchids and also for dog violets, meadow rues, and yellow avens. Another popular destination is the nine-mile drive up the western slopes of Brockway Mountain. At more than seven hundred feet above the lakeshore, the mountain top supports a hardy mix of stunted oak, birch, and jack pine, as well as yarrows, hawkweeds, buttercups, and oxeye daisies, all of which must be capable of enduring shallow soils and fierce, desiccating winds.

The Superior coastline forms yet another distinct environment, and several small roadside parks make it easy to explore. The exposed coastal bedrock ranges from dark gray, wave-smoothed basalt to roughly textured shelves of red brown conglomerate and local concentrations of sandstone. The various rock types offer habitat choices in their own right. Shore flowers do best on the basalt outcrops, which support scattered wild roses, cinquefoils, and junipers as well as trees such as birch and red pine. Being more vulnerable to storm waves, the low-lying areas of sandstone are less generous in their display of vegetation, and the conglomerate shelves, which often rise out of the nearshore water at steep angles, are almost bare.

I do my best to sample a range of natural environments. Before starting for home early Sunday afternoon, I set out on the short one-and-a-half-mile hike through the Keweenaw Shore and Lake Upson nature sanctuaries. The trail enters the forest on the south side of route M-26, no more than a hundred feet from the lake. As I enter the shade of the forest, the air feels cool and slightly damp. Generous strands of old man's beard that hang from balsam branches, cedars and birches, moss-covered logs and boulders, assorted ferns, and profuse carpets of wild ginger containing incredibly large leaves attest to the rich, moist soils that form in low-lying areas and the abundant growth that frequent fog and lake-effect rains produce. A bit farther into the forest, large patches of thimbleberries and bunchberries begin to surround the trail.

Before long, the red pines and the small flowers that grow in their shade become more abundant. Red pines impose demanding conditions on understory plants, which must be able to tolerate low levels of direct light as well as the acidic soils that form from a thick ground layer of slowly decomposing needles. Moreover, red pine stands are vulnerable to fire and depend on it to regenerate. If understory plants are to form large patches and retain their presence over time, they have to be able to survive disturbance. Not surprisingly, red pines favor lakeshores, peninsulas, and islands where blocked by water, fires spare enough mature trees to allow regeneration to take place. The cool temperatures, high winds, and abbreviated summers of such places present additional challenges to understory plants.

With their slender crowns and branch-free lower trunks, mature red pines often form fairly open stands, allowing plants that require moderate light levels to grow in less densely shaded areas. The shade and fire tolerance of plants in the pine understory varies. Some, such as the bunchberry, fare better than others in low light, but as a general rule, although most of the plants tolerate moderate shade, they grow better in more open areas. Their ability to withstand fire displays greater variation. At one extreme is again the bunchberry, which like many other successful pine forest plants, relies on long, woody underground rhizomes to survive all but very hot flames. At the other is the twinflower, whose thin, aboveground stems are easily killed by even low-intensity fires. Yet it and other fire sensitive plants have been at less of a reproductive disadvantage during the past century of human fire suppression.

Fire tolerant or not, the twinflower grows well in cool, acidic

pine-stand soils. Linnaeus much admired this tiny pink member
of the Honeysuckle family, having his portrait painted with it
and wanting to see it named *Linnaea borealis* in his honor; it has
become as much an emblem of his legacy as of its boreal forest
habitat. It is easy to see why the twinflower was the eighteenth-
century botanist's favorite. Its small fragrant blossoms are delicate
and unassuming, and each lasts only about a week. The blossoms
are borne in pairs on thin upright stalks that rise no more than
a few inches from the long, creeping woody stems to which they
are attached. The stems are trimmed and almost hidden by closely
spaced pairs of shiny evergreen leaves, and bedecked with their
nodding pink bells, they trail like garland over moss-covered logs
and boulders on the forest floor.

Many of the flowers with which the twinflower shares its
ground-level haunts are much more sparingly distributed, or
less likely to grow profusely in the places where they are found.
Such is the case with the starflower, one of the few pine associates
that, in my view, comes close to matching the simple elegance of
Linnaeus's pink-colored favorite. It shares the twinflower's preference for shady and moist habitats in mixed and coniferous stands,
and reflecting its similar circumpolar range, it also carries the
species name *borealis,* "of the north." It is, in its own way, equally
unique, for it belongs to the rare class of seven-petaled flowers.
Its tiny white blossoms, which are borne either singly or in pairs
above a whorl of thin pointed leaves, can have anywhere from five
to nine petals. Yet on many specimens, the starlike appearance
from which the plant takes its common name is produced by seven
finely pointed white petals. These seven petals are often accompanied by the even rarer combination of seven stamens and seven
sepals. I see only a single starflower specimen during my hike.

About half a mile into the forest, the trail begins to cross hillier
terrain, where there are more frequent changes in habitat. Up
slope, the soils become thinner, sandier, and rockier, and scattered
areas of pebble-laden conglomerate break through the surface.
There seems to be a flower for every habitat along the trail. The

poor soils and the sunshine that reaches through large gaps in the canopy do little to deter another common pine associate, the pipsissewa. The pipsissewa can grow in a variety of soil types, but it is often found in sandier and drier areas where few other flowers grow—fewer yet can match the appeal of its waxy, rose-tinted blossoms. Like many other north woods plants, it had a number of medicinal uses in native America. One of these, to break down gall and kidney stones, gave rise to its unusual common name, which comes from a Cree word meaning "it breaks into small pieces." If the common name draws attention to one of the pipsissewa's practical uses, the scientific name, *Chimaphila umbellata,* serves, exactly as Linnaeus intended his Latin binomial nomenclature would, as a helpful tool in the plant's identification. *Chimaphila,* the genus name, comes from the Greek words for "winter lover" and is a reference to the evergreen leaves that encircle the plant's slender stem. The species name, *umbellata,* alludes to the loose cluster, or umbel, that is formed by its five-petaled blossoms that when open, nod and radiate outward from the stem in an umbrella-like fashion. Unfortunately, the flower clusters on the trailside plant have yet to open.

The pipsissewa is a member of the Wintergreen family. Wintergreens have a fairly distinctive appearance, with whorls of thick, shiny evergreen leaves, nodding buds, and fragrant, waxy, disk-shaped flowers that usually have five petals and five sepals. Several of the family's genera appear in the northern forest. Among them is the *Pyrola* genus, which is represented by a handful of species, each of which displays a slightly different habitat preference. Thus, while the nodding, or common, pyrola is mainly found in drier areas, the pink pyrola prefers the wet, limey soils frequently associated with white cedar groves. Pyrolas are popularly referred to as shinleafs, a name that, like pipsissewa, reflects the plant's medicinal use by Native Americans, who made a plaster for treating wounds and lesions out of its leaves.

Unlike the pipsissewa and shinleaf, not all plants popularly called wintergreens belong to the Wintergreen family, a fact that underscores the confusion that can result from the use of non-scientific names. One plant that is not an authentic wintergreen but is rather a member of the Heath family is the low, woody so-called wintergreen shrub, which grows in dry, shady soils in the red pine forest. The shrub is often admired for its tiny, white late-summer flowers and its red autumn berries, which hang on well into the following summer.

Another wintergreen impostor, one whose bright purple flowers are hard to miss, is the fringed polygala, or flowering wintergreen. The fringed polygala prefers rich, moist habitats such as the shady trailside depression where I encounter my only specimen. It is also popularly called "gaywings" in reference to the winglike appearance created by two sepals that extend laterally from the top of the flower. Three petals, at the bottom of which is a fringed or crested lower lip, join in the shape of a tube below the two sepals, giving the flower a distinctly orchidlike look. If the name of flowering wintergreen suggests a false association with the Wintergreen family, the name of fringed polygala provides a surprisingly accurate indication, at least as far as nonscientific designations go, of the *Polygala* genus and the Polygalaceae, or Milkwort family, to which the plant belongs. The Latin *Polygala* comes from the Greek words for "much" and "milk," reflecting the once-held belief that milkworts increased lactation in cows and nursing mothers.

After crossing Brockway Mountain Drive, the trail descends toward a cool, shady streamside habitat. Nearly hidden among the mosses, I find three specimens of one of the most enchanting north woods plants, the one-flowered wintergreen. What better name than *Moneses uniflora,* "single delight," to describe the allure of this tiny, shade-loving flower of mossy coniferous places. A true wintergreen, it is the sole member of the *Moneses,* or "Delight," genus, and as both its common and scientific names suggest, each plant has only a single nodding flower. The flower can easily be recognized by the distinctive-looking green stigmas that appear on each of its five white petals. Yet, absent this blossom, the one-flowered wintergreen can be exceedingly difficult to spot. It is only three or four inches tall, and its small basal leaves are usually well hidden in the moss.

There are other challenges in locating one-flowered wintergreens. Many specimens are actually fertilized without flowering and thus lack a blossom. The blossoms of those that do flower are very short-lived, opening for only a week within a limited window of time in late June or early July. Moreover, as is the case along the trail, in most places where it grows in the forest, the one-flowered wintergreen is confined to one or a few specimens. Its ephemeral beauty easily eludes even the most devoted of admirers. It seems only fitting to use the additional common name of "wood nymph" when referring to this diminutive, moss-dwelling white maiden.

The trail crosses a stream to join the Lake Upson Nature Sanctuary loop by means of a few slender, haphazardly strewn logs; I suspect that the hiker responsible for laying down the logs reached the opposite bank with feet no drier than my own. The Upson trail traverses fairly level ground through a mixed forest of spruce, fir, birch, red oak, sugar maple, and beech. Many of these trees have considerably more demanding soil, moisture, and temperature requirements than their pine forest counterparts. Sheltered by the ridge from the worst of the desiccating off-lake winds and favored by the slightly warmer air and deeper soils that gather in the valley, deciduous trees are able to dominate the Lake Upson canopy. Unlike the needle carpets common to pine stands, the rapidly decomposing leaves produce a deep, fertile bed of mineral-rich duff for flowers. Yet deciduous forest flowers, like the trees in whose understory they grow, have stiffer reproductive requirements. In particular, they need lots of sunlight, which means that they have to bloom quickly before the trees come fully into leaf in late spring. In sharp contrast to the Keweenaw Shore trail, in late June the floral display along the Lake Upson loop is practically nonexistent.

There are, however, other intriguing ground-dwelling plants, including one of my favorites, the stiff clubmoss. Large clubmoss patches grow in the leafy duff in moist, shady areas. The stiff clubmoss is, not surprisingly, a member of the Clubmoss, or *Lycopodium,* genus. It often grows in spreading colonies, with each of its slender, vertical aboveground stems carrying a single spore-bearing cone, or "club." Yet like other clubmoss species, it is not actually a moss but a nonflowering vascular plant. Club-mosses have a lilliputian appearance, and as the common names of plants such as the ground pine and ground cedar suggest, they resemble miniature evergreens. Looking down at short stems barely the height of my boot, I find it hard to imagine that three billion years ago in the tropics of the Paleozoic, the ancestors of the clubmosses grew as tall as trees, their decomposed remains piling up, along with those of giant ferns and horsetails, to form the earth's ancient coal beds.

A particularly large and seemingly familiar patch of clubmoss about halfway around the loop leads me to think that I may have missed the spur trail back out to the stream bank. I usually locate at least a few memorable features by which to regain my bearings should I become disoriented while on a trail, but the Lake Upson loop has offered few distinctive flowers or other obvious markers. The clubmoss patches are largely indistinguishable from one another except by their size, but since the possibility of losing my way on a loop trail had never occurred to me, I have not paid close attention to such variations. To ensure that the Lake Upson, Keweenaw Shore, and other sanctuaries it oversees remain in their natural state, the Michigan Nature Association performs only minimal trail maintenance, and the need to circumvent frequent snags and downed trunks makes it easy to lose sight of the blue markers on the trees. It takes another pass around the loop and a car on Brockway Mountain Drive to clue me into the direction I need to go, and after abandoning the trail to shortcut through the forest, I quickly reach the stream bank. I only have to backtrack a dozen feet or so to see that a large snag would have made it almost impossible to relocate the spur trail from the loop.

Driving south on the peninsula an hour later, I reflect on the serendipity of my decision to scrap my initial plans and spend the weekend exploring natural places. I feel especially fortunate to have encountered such a rewarding floral display in the Keweenaw Shore and Lake Upson sanctuaries. Given the better than expected weather, the change in plans was an easy choice. Yet around the lake, well-laid plans are just as likely thwarted by a sudden turn in weather or by the discovery that wildflower and other seasonal displays fail to occur when predicted. It is best not to wrap one's hopes too tightly around a specific agenda. More often than not, having a grab bag of options comes in handy when exploring the Superior region.

Orion

IT IS MID-NOVEMBER AND DUSK HAS FALLEN BY FIVE
o'clock. I remove my gloves and lean my hands against the bare
rock. The sky and waters surround me in the fading light like
a vast amphitheater in which the sound of each wave, rising,
bowing its crest, and then crashing headlong, assaults the silence
and repose of the shore. I can still feel the residual warmth of the
sun's rays on the rock, the rock struggling to hold on to day and
lightness. I am waiting for the constellation Orion to appear on
the southeastern horizon, searching the early winter sky for the
meaning of a human life that is slipping away. Like the warm
and secure grasp of a trusted friend, the rock under my palms
anchors me deep in that place where the pain and loneliness of
life become bearable, and as dusk turns quietly to night, I watch
the stars unfold.

For nearly six millennia of recorded history, people have looked
for constellations in the nighttime sky, finding in the dark vault
of the heavens the gods, animals, and heroes that have populated
their myths and carried them through the cycles of birth and

rebirth, the death and renewal, that all life brings. In a world of perils and unknowns, celestial bodies moved predictably overhead. Surviving artifacts and structures suggest that people used the stars as navigational and practical aids, timed the events of their seasonal cycle with the movements of celestial bodies, and aligned mounds, monuments, and ceremonial centers with the stars, sun, and planets. Yet, they provide only scattered clues to the real meaning the universe held, to the unrecorded thoughts and observations, countless intimate reflections and connections that individuals brought to their experience of the celestial realm.

I like to imagine that then, as now, people looked to the heavens to bring order to the universe and purpose to the inexplicable events of which lives are shaped. That when my ancient forebears looked up at the early winter sky, they were, like me, searching for the answers out of which new understandings and possibilities are born. That then, as now, the different answers they found, and the varied explanations and practices they accepted became a basis for the shared outlooks and experiences through which communities are sustained.

Orion seems to have featured prominently in the lives and myths of many early societies. The brightest constellation in the nighttime sky, it is easy to identify and was used, along with other natural indicators, to track the seasons on whose prediction survival depended. In the northern hemisphere, a twilight rising of Orion foretells the coming of winter, a predawn sighting the onset of midsummer, frequently with its life-sustaining rains. The ancient Egyptians believed that Orion held the departed soul of Osiris, the god of fertility and the afterlife, who appears on the walls of temples and tombs along with his wife, Isis, her soul at rest in the star Sirius. They used the first predawn sighting of Sirius, which, rising a few weeks after Orion, is the sky's brightest star, to predict the flooding of the Nile, whose banks they farmed, and to mark the start of a new 365-day calendar year. And in building the main burial chamber of the Great Pyramid at Giza more than four and a half millennia ago, they aligned the southern shaft, through which the dead pharaoh's soul would pass to the afterlife, with Orion's belt.

Orion also appears as a god, creator, and giver of fertility among the ancient Maya, who saw in its stars the form of their first father and the god of maize, as well as the smoke and three-stoned hearth of the fire of creation that he had lit. Hindu mythology associates the constellation with the creator of the universe, Prajápati, who appears in the sky in the form of a deer. And for the ancient Greeks, who provided many of the myths associated with the constellations in Western society today, as well as for the Norsemen and many Native American cultures, Orion's stars contained the figure of a great hunter.

Like early peoples the world over, Native Americans often opened their doors to the east, where the sun and the constellations rose, and aligned their homes with the four cardinal directions. Symbols of celestial bodies and records of astronomical events appear in the rock art of the Navajo, Anasazi, Chumash, and others, as well as on lodges, tepees, masks, and headdresses across North America. While the sun, moon, and planets are believed to have been more common in the timing of seasonal and ceremonial events, stars appear frequently in myths and stories, imparting moral and practical lessons. According to the creation myths of many Iroquoian and Algonquin-speaking communities, the first humans emerged from the stars, descending to earth through a hole in the sky. Stories of traditional Ojibwe beliefs tell of people gaining spiritual insight through dream journeys to the celestial realm.

Some nine thousand years ago, the first inhabitants of this region may have sat, like me, on Lake Superior's rocky shore searching the early winter sky for signs of Orion's arrival. By the time these Paleo-Indians arrived, the glaciers were firmly in retreat. The landscape they encountered was stark and windswept, dominated by bare rock and permafrost, and save for islands of cold-tolerant black spruce, vegetation was confined to patchy areas of moss, grass, and tundra plants. Large glacial lakes and rivers crossed the earth. The Superior basin was filled with meltwaters but was still bordered to the north by a huge wall of shrinking ice. The basin's waters reached hundreds of feet higher than they do today, and the region's early inhabitants lived and hunted far inland of the present shoreline.

Perhaps they were daunted by what they saw, but they stayed on to fashion survival out of the harsh and desolate earth. They hunted bison, caribou, and moose with stone-pointed spears, and possibly also mammoths, mastodons, musk oxen, and other big game. They gathered what little in the way of roots, berries, bulbs, and other edibles the land had to offer, but apart from fluted spear points and scattered campsites along lakes, streams, and the old Superior shorelines, they left few artifacts or remains to inform us of their daily lives.

Ever on the move across the unsettled earth, these small, migratory bands may have returned seasonally to familiar places. Over time, they likely developed attachments, the kind born of years of sentiment and experience, to the features of the land. Perhaps the immensity of the land and the relentless vulnerability they shared upon it also drew them closer to those with whom they wandered. And perhaps when they from time to time encountered other small groups, they felt a semblance of the community of humans to which they belonged.

Sometime around eight thousand years ago, the region's climate gradually started to become more forgiving. As northerly migrating red and white pine and fir and birch moved in, the big game died out, and the postglacial lakes and rivers gradually receded. The warming continued, and eventually oaks and prairie grasses moved in south and west of the lake, and even in former tundra lands, a greater variety of deciduous trees and shrubs arrived. These changes brought new food sources: deer, elk, birds, and other small mammals as well as an increase in fish and seeds, roots, and berries. Harpoon points and fishhooks, traps, snares, and the tools with which dugout canoes were made begin to make their appearance in the archaeological record.

People continued to wander with the seasons, but they now lived with greater knowledge of what their environment had to offer. Eventually, they also began to harvest wild rice, tap sugar maples for sap, and grow maize and squash, all of which provided food for denser populations and more settled lifestyles. Semi-sedentary villages or seasonal camps emerged, especially in the mixed forests south and inland of the lake where farming took hold. Along the lakeshore, communities that dispersed into family groupings to hunt and trap farther inland in winter came together to fish, gather, and tend small gardens in villages around the mouths of rivers in summer. Localized adaptations to the landscape and greater cultural and technological sophistication emerged. By twenty-five hundred years ago, the development of increasingly complex tools and implements as well as clay pottery, weaving, and new ceremonial practices had made life both richer and less arduous. New opportunities arose to form deeper attach-ments to people and places. As communities became imbued with a greater sense of security and belonging, routines and rituals were anchored in the abiding features of a familiar landscape.

As their skill base expanded, people who lived around the lake began to make use of other resources whose potential had previously gone unrecognized. Sometime between four and five thousand years ago, they developed the first metal culture of North America. They found copper nuggets in the glacial debris—glaciers had plucked the nuggets out of veins and vesicles in the lava—and also quarried the red metal extensively on Isle Royale and on Michigan's Upper Peninsula. Prehistoric mining relied mainly on spalling, heating the surrounding rock with fire and then dousing it with cold water to promote cracking to free the metal. Yet native miners also used hammer stones of hard lava rock to chip away at the softer bedrock in which the copper lay. Mining operations around the lake were possibly extensive. It is thought that several hundred thousand pounds of copper, at a minimum, may have been excavated. Because the copper was almost pure, it was soft and could be easily shaped into blades, fishhooks, harpoon points, knives, and other tools. It was also traded throughout eastern North America and, some have suggested, south to the Aztecs and Incas. For reasons not entirely clear, large-scale mining around the lake died out a little over three thousand years ago. The region's native inhabitants never worked iron or produced alloys, such as bronze, with which they could have made stronger tools and weapons.

The loosely knit bands of people that we know today as the Ojibwe continued the ancient pattern of forging beliefs and customs out of the features of the land. Their annual cycle was finely attuned, with local variations, to reap the most of what each season had to offer, and migrating westward around Superior's shores beginning in the latter 1600s, they developed an intimate knowledge of what the region's lakes, rivers, and forests could provide. They covered their dwellings with birch bark and reeds, shaped bows out of oak and ash, gathered mosses for bedding and diapers, and used almost every tree and flower—wild rose and pea, goldenrod, tansy, bush honeysuckle, fir, alder, willow, sumac, poplar, the list is nearly endless—to treat wounds, headaches, and other ailments.

Along the lake's rugged, conifer-dominated northern shore, where population densities were low, family groups lived in small bands, hunting, fishing, and gathering. South and west of the lake, maple sugar formed an important dietary staple for many communities. In early spring, usually before the snow had melted, family groups that had spent the winter apart united around the "sugar bush." The sap was tapped, and after having been reduced to syrup through boiling, stirred until granulated or poured into molds to harden into sugar cakes, which could be stored for use as a seasoning and source of energy throughout the year. During the summer and fall, people generally came together in larger communities around bays, river mouths, and lakeshores, strengthening and passing on through shared rituals and stories their connections to one another and to the places to which they returned to. In the meantime, food stores had to be built up for the coming winter. The men fished and snared fowl, rabbits, and other game, while the women tended small gardens and gathered wild roots, nuts, and berries, drying and storing surpluses that would carry them through the winter when game was scarce. In the forests of Minnesota and Wisconsin, wild rice was also harvested from shallow lakes and marshes toward the season's end. As the winter gradually approached, the villages began to break up, and secure in the web of customs and commitments that community life had affirmed, families repaired to their hunting camps to prepare for the coming of winter.

Northern native peoples, I used to think, must have dreaded the arrival of Orion, a harbinger of cold and darkness, in the nighttime sky. Yet, apparently they found reason to celebrate the coming of all seasons, including winter, when beavers and otters came into prime and hunters could pursue deer across the ice. Perhaps, during the longest nights of the year, with little but the moon and the stars and a small fire to light their world, they too found comfort in Orion's bright stars.

Through the spear points, pots, knives, mines, and other artifacts they left behind, as well as the beliefs and customs they continue to pass on, countless generations of people around the lake have recorded how life changed with the climate as the glacial age drifted further back in human recollection. The harsh lives they endured and the perils of the lands they encountered are the stuff of textbooks, possible to intellectually comprehend but, for most of us, never really to grasp. Today, towns and roads cross once empty landscapes, and modern science affords much of the security that eluded societies in the past. Night no longer brings the arch of impenetrable darkness across which the souls of gods once strode.

Yet whether we see them or not, the shapes of the beasts and heroes that populated the myths of our forebears still rest in the nighttime sky. Modern astronomy has done little to change the constellations identified through millennia of human observation. The twelve constellations of the zodiac were plotted twenty-five hundred years ago by the priest-astronomers of the Babylonians, who farmed the banks of the Euphrates River in what is now Iraq. Through compiling and studying Babylonian and earlier Greek records, including that of the Greek astronomer Hipparchus, the second-century Egyptian mathematician Ptolemy plotted more than a thousand stars and identified over half of the eighty-eight presently recognized constellations. It later fell to ninth- and tenth-century Muslim astronomers to translate, revise, and build on Greek works while Europe languished in the Dark Ages. In the process, Greek star names were translated into Arabic. Arabic star names, in turn, were later translated or Latinized by European astronomers. The names of Orion's brightly glowing stars Rigel and Betelgeuse as well as the lesser luminaries Saiph, Mintaka, Alnilam, and Alnitak all originate with the Arabic.

The northern night contains bright lights of another kind, whose strange, random displays inspired legends of life and fears of doom in ancient societies. Lake Superior lies at the outer reaches of the so-called auroral oval, a big irregularly shaped circumpolar band of frequent auroral displays that dips south around Hudson Bay. Ojibwe saw the northern lights as fires that burned in the lodges of their ancestors, as dancing spirits, or the lit-up path upon which souls walked. I saw my first aurora display in late August two years ago, looking out over the lake at the brink of dawn. Faint but unmistakable, luminous sheets of white surged like wind-driven clouds from far down the western horizon while in the eastern sky, the last star in the Big Dipper's tail had just begun to fade in a thin band of pale light. Green, pink, or white, giant lights that dart frantically in the darkness have had to be explained throughout history, be it with reference to charged particles, angry gods, or ancestral fires. Whether with fear, hope, vulnerability, or wonder, had I lived a thousand or even a hundred years ago, I think I would have had to multiply many times over the thoughts and feelings spawned by the mysteries of the nighttime sky.

As the quest to unravel these mysteries continues, astronomers have looked to Orion to understand the process by which new stars emerge. Orion contains the brightest nebula in the sky and the only one that is visible to the unaided eye. Despite its fuzzy appearance, this glowing cloud of mostly hydrogen gas was mistaken for an ordinary star until the French lawyer Nicholas Peiresc first viewed it through a telescope in 1610. Unfortunately, Peiresc's work, as well as the independent discovery one year later by the Swiss Jesuit astronomer Johann Baptist Cysatus, remained buried for several centuries. As a result, the Dutchman Christiaan Huygens has commonly received credit for his 1656 discovery of the Orion nebula.

It is to the English court astronomer Sir William Herschel, however, that we owe most of our early knowledge of the Orion nebula. A musician by training, Herschel built large reflecting telescopes to see far into the sky, and aided by his sister Caroline, he spent two decades systematically searching for new nebulae. On March 4, 1774, he pointed his telescope at the Orion nebula. Comparing what he saw with earlier drawings, he concluded that the nebula's appearance had changed. The nebula, he predicted, seemed "fit to produce a star by its condensation." He later suggested that gravity caused diffuse, rotating clouds of gas in the universe to gradually condense into nebulae, whose size and brightness continued to change as condensation progressed.

Nebulae, astronomers have confirmed, serve as giant wombs, birthing new stars out of the gravity-induced collapse of a cloud of rotating particles in their midst. Orion's stellar newborns are among the youngest additions to the galaxy and radiate enough light to make the constellation's most famous nebula glow, though not without plenty of help from several older, much hotter stars. The light of each new star dissipates the gas that surrounds it, eventually creating a hole in the cloud through which its light can be seen. As star formation proceeds and more gas is dispersed, a nebula grows progressively more diffuse until it eventually disappears. In its place, hundreds, thousands, or even hundreds of thousands of new stars begin to chart their course

across the heavens, the lights of the future emerging out of amor-
phous matter.

And so it was with this land. Great sheets of ice melted into
water and vanished. In their place came trees and animals and
eventually the region's earliest human inhabitants. People who
may have sat, like me, on Lake Superior's shore at dusk searching
the early winter sky for signs of Orion's arrival. I wonder what
possibilities they saw.

On the Porcupine Coast

FEW AREAS AROUND LAKE SUPERIOR OFFER AS LARGE
a contrast in natural environments as does Porcupine Mountains
Wilderness State Park on the northwestern edge of Michigan's
Upper Peninsula. On the lakeshore, waves and sun rays stroke
the smooth backs of sandstone shelves. The shelves contain
some of the most visually stunning patterns and designs I have
seen on rocks anywhere, ancient motifs framed like paintings in
nature's gallery, and the features underfoot are what catch the
eye. The situation could not be more different on the forested
hillsides inland of the lake, where old-growth hemlocks rise like
giant relics of a world that loggers nearly took the last of. The
park supports the largest old-growth northern hardwood forest
in North America. The hemlocks' canopies cloak the forest floor
in perpetual shade, and plant cover and animal life are meager. It
is the solemn stillness of furrowed trunks and gracefully draping
branches that draws me in. Shade and silence, light and rhythm.
The contrast is like night and day, and I pile one on top of the
other like a layered sandwich during my visits.

I always start out on the lakeshore, walking west from the Union Bay campground on the park's eastern edge. Once the campground is out of sight, I rarely meet other people. For as far as I walk, I can have the shoreline to myself. Red brown sandstone shelves incline gently toward the water. The shelves are narrow and low-lying. For the most part, their surfaces are as flat as boards, but in a few places they have shallow bowl-shaped depressions. In sheltered areas, the ground is littered with slabs and broken pieces. Large slabs, which can be the size of windowpanes, shift uneasily and look as if they are about to break under my step. Most of the slabs are thin, no more than two or three inches, and have the saturated red brown, iron oxide tint of the surrounding shelves. Occasionally, however, I come across a piece that is light tan or ochre-colored.

Like sacred stone tablets, these sandstone shelves record the ancient events that have shaped the Porcupine coast. They are part of the Copper Harbor Conglomerate, a formation of mostly sandstone and conglomerate that sits at the base of a sequence of rocks known as the Oronto Group. The sequence, which extends in an arch from Michigan's Keweenaw Peninsula southwestward into northern Wisconsin, also includes the Nonesuch Shale and the Freda Sandstone, which can be seen in other areas of the park. Sediments that make up the Copper Harbor Conglomerate were eroded from volcanic highlands after lavas had stopped flowing from the midcontinental rift. Because the landscape began to erode even before the volcanism ended, the formation also includes some "traps" of basalt. Once eroded, the sediments were carried by huge, braided streams northward into the Superior basin, and over millions of years the fluvial deposits built up. Eventually, they became buried deep underground, where they were compacted and cemented, only to later be exposed by uplift and erosion.

Small, broken-off pieces as well as huge slabs display gently undulating, wave-formed ripple marks from the stream beds on which the sediments were deposited. There are also mud cracks that formed when wet, silty deposits dried out. As land plants had yet to take hold, and runoff waters flowed quickly over the landscape, the water levels in ancient streams fluctuated widely. During periods with little runoff, muddy sediment along the rivers' banks dried out and cracked. When water levels later rose, iron-rich silts and sands sometimes settled in the cracks and tinted them dark brown. The pieces in between the cracks, however, retained the lighter, redder color of the muddy sediments. In the style of mosaics, darker outlines surround the paler red pieces like grout around tiles.

The difference in color can be even more dramatic. In isolated areas, it is the cracks that are red brown while the pieces in between them, usually eroded mud chips, are light tan. In a process geologists call reduction, oxygen-poor waters flowing through the rock acted like a bleaching fluid, removing iron oxide and thus color from the pieces but not from the cracks. Water flowing over and through the land left more than ripple marks and mud cracks. Groundwater that moved through pores in the rock also precipitated the mineral calcite. Today, white calcite chips and veinlets adorn the sandstone shelves like mother-of-pearl insets.

Not only pattern and design but also texture are on display on the Porcupines' shore. In most places, the sandstone is matte, without much luster, and just grainy enough to feel like a piece of fine sandpaper. Here and there, however, it has a smooth, shiny lavender surface that resembles the glaze on a ccramic dish. In other areas, the sandstone gives way to massive layers of roughly textured conglomerate, whose hundreds of variously derived and colored pebbles have been cemented together in a matrix of sand and clay. Occasional boulders of conglomerate can also be seen scattered about like leftover construction concrete. And for added decoration, higher up on the shore the rock is covered with dense patches of gray and white crustose lichens. The lichens form intricate designs of dime-sized circles and floral-shaped rosettes with lacy outlines. Like squares on a quilt, the patterns and textures change where cracks fragment the rock.

Save for in a few sheltered areas, the ground cover on the rock is scant. Common yarrows, panicled asters, harebells, flowering ninebark, wild rose, and an occasional meadow rue and white campion grow in soil-filled cracks. But the sandstone is heavily chipped, and given the constant shifting of the slabs, soils have little time to build up. The low-lying rock, moreover, becomes wet and slippery with even small waves on the lake, and few of the shelves are wide enough to allow shrubs and grasses to safely take hold. Some of the driftwood logs that line the upper shore as well as the trunks of living trees are partly buried by cobbles that storm waves have pushed all the way to the forest's edge.

I still find it hard to believe that this narrow stretch of coastline holds such a treasure trove of rock-born textures and designs. During my first visits to the park, I was unaware of the shoreline's riches and spent most of my time on forested trails farther inland. I recall hiking a segment of the Lake Superior trail and looking down at the coastal plain from a ledge high above the water. From so far away, the low-land canopy appeared to lead right up to the lake, and the sandstone shelves were too narrow to be seen.

If only the coast were wider, the patterns on the rock would be more plentiful. How many of these attractive motifs, I have often wondered, lie hidden under the forested soils that begin a bare twenty feet from the lake, or deep beneath the churning waters. Unfortunately, people have also carved names and figures into some of the most interesting rocks, which happen to lie within a few minutes walk of the Union Bay campground. Yet there are still enough that I seem to find at least one new motif each time I visit the park.

Come midday, when the sun beats down on the unsheltered coast, I follow a trail into the hemlock forest near the mouth of the Presque Isle River on the park's western edge. The light-filled world beyond grows progressively more distant. The forest's soils are dark and moist, in many places puddle-ridden, and my feet quickly become wet from the dirty splashes of jumps that fall short of their target. It is some comfort to know that this damp, rich environment made it difficult for postlogging fires, which often decimated surviving pine and boreal stands elsewhere, to spread far and fast in the Porcupine Mountains forest. Moist soils, moreover, are precisely what hemlocks need to grow best. Following the glaciers' retreat, hemlocks were slower to spread north than other evergreens, such as spruce, that were better adapted to growing in the poor soils that initially developed on top of the glacial till. They thrive especially well on cool and moist north-facing slopes overlooking the lake, as well as in valleys and ravines that capture run-off from higher ground.

Hemlocks are long-lived, often reaching three or four hundred years, and as a stand matures, the growing environment underneath becomes increasingly inhospitable for plants and other trees, few of which can tolerate the lack of light or the acidic soils formed by decomposing needles. Ground cover consists mainly of bracken fern, wild sarsaparilla, occasional clumps of Indian pipe, and other low-light vegetation. The exception is in sun-lit clearings where large trees have been downed by the wind. Because hemlocks have fairly shallow root systems, there are many of these clearings, and trunks and snags litter the ground. Thimbleberries thrive in the openings. So do hemlock saplings, which if need be, can wait patiently on a rotting moss-covered stump for decades before a windthrow opens up the canopy and provides the light for them to grow. Yellow birch seedlings also do well in the rich soils around decaying logs, and sugar maple saplings blanket the ground in sun-filled clearings. Sugar maples are avid seed producers, and compared to hemlocks, their fast-growing seedlings take a more aggressive reproductive tack. Neither tree's strategy is foolproof, however. Competition for sunlight is fierce, and few seedlings make it to maturity.

Entering the forest, I do not at first notice the silence, or realize that there is so little to listen to. Near the trailhead, the rushing of the Presque Isle River over its dark gray bed of shale fills the forest, and the flutelike melodies of a hermit thrush carry from a distance. Like a song from the past, the melodies play on in my mind long after the music has faded, beautiful, jarring notes that resound with loss and hope. And so it was for the hermit thrush, for whom the destruction and later protection of the old-growth forest meant the near disappearance and then the partial reclamation of its habitat. Once the notes fade, the only steady sound comes from my boots sinking and squeezing water out of the muddy soils. When I stop to look around, the silence hits me with the force of a sonic boom that fails to materialize. It is the stillness of uncontested life, of a growing environment in which hemlocks reign supreme, leaving little room for deciduous trees and shrubs, whose nuts and seeds attract the birds and small mammals that bring woods to life with activity and song. I wonder if before making their first cuts, the loggers ever leaned back hard against the brown, furrowed bark of an old hemlock tree and listened to the silence.

Life is by no means completely absent from the forest; it is merely less abundant than in more open woods. White-tailed deer thrive on the hemlocks' needles and often overwinter in stands close to the lake. Barred owls, blackburnian warblers, and winter wrens make their homes in the branches, as do red squirrels. Porcupines nibble away at the tops of the trunks, and the holes of pileated woodpeckers, drummed in a long line one on top of the other, join together in the shapes of dugout canoes in dead trees, leaving impressive chip piles on the ground. Like that of the hermit thrush, the fate of the pileated woodpecker rests with the old-growth forest, where carpenter ants infest soft, rotting wood of dying trees. Two of these massive black birds fly silently across the trail some thirty feet in front of me. Yet except for the scolding of a squirrel, I neither see nor hear much of the forest's other residents.

About two miles out, the trail skirts a hill of young sugar maples. From the hemlocks' dimly lit stands, the maples' smooth gray trunks look aglow with light. Warm sunshine filters through the canopy, and the setting is airy, almost playful. With deep, branching root systems, sugar maples grow best in thick, loamy soils and favor sheltered southern hillsides, which capture sunshine as well as wind-strewn leaves and debris. While choosy about their location, they replenish the earth each fall with an ample store of nutrient-rich leaves. In the bounty of light and the rich duff of the maples' litter, life abounds, and a generous assortment of Dutchman's breeches, bracken ferns, and blue-bead lilies blankets the ground. The hierarchy of shade and silence that will come as the maples mature and extend their canopies has yet to be established.

According to the park map, the trail winds close enough to the lakeshore in several places to allow for a side foray. This, I soon discover, looks deceptively easy on the map. Steep, sandy bluffs separate the forest from the coast, and in most places it is impossible to see from the trail whether a reasonably safe descent can be made. In the one place where coastal access looks possible, at the mouth of Speakers Creek, a rental cabin is visible through the trees, and a park service sign requests that hikers respect the privacy of cabin stayers by venturing no farther toward the lake. Seeing no obvious respite from the damp, dark understory of centuries of old growth, I turn around and head back out to the trailhead. The clear skies of late afternoon bode well for watching the sun set from the wave-washed shore at Union Bay. Light and rhythm, what is in short supply in the ancient stands of hemlock. That is what I need.

The Mission of Saint Esprit

IN 1665, FATHER CLAUDE JEAN ALLOUEZ BUILT A birch-bark chapel on the southeastern shore of Chequamegon Bay. La Pointe du Saint Esprit was the first Jesuit mission on Lake Superior. Allouez has sometimes been called the "Founder of Catholicism" in North America, and as evidence of his labors, he carefully recorded the number of baptisms he performed. Yet the Jesuits generally found it difficult to sustain the faith of their converts, and seventeenth-century French Catholicism failed to sink deep roots among Native Americans. Allouez and many other early fathers were, however, curious and adventuresome men, not easily deterred by the hardship and isolation of wilderness life. Having carried their faith across the Atlantic, they ventured deep into America's unexplored hinterlands. They traveled widely, spoke Indian languages, and made detailed journal entries on Native American life and customs and on the geography, flora, and fauna of the regions in which they served. While there is no easy way to evaluate the legacy of missionary endeavors, the Jesuits hold many firsts in the annals of European exploration and discovery in North America.

In 1667, Allouez became the first white man to complete the circumnavigation of Lake Superior. The geographical knowledge he acquired provided the basis, along with native reports obtained by Father Claude Dablon, for a map that when published in the *Jesuit Relations* of 1670–71, offered the most accurate representation of the lake available. Through his contacts with the Indians, Allouez also became the earliest European known to have used the name *Mes-sipi* to refer to the Great River of which natives spoke. He reported being shown copper ingots by the Indians and seeing the metal on the lake bottom, confirming long-standing rumors heard by French explorers since Jacques Cartier's arrival in 1536 about the presence of copper in the area. Disseminated to European readers and preserved for future historians through the *Jesuit Relations,* Allouez's lay endeavors vastly expanded European knowledge of the Lake Superior region.

Other Jesuit fathers likewise contributed to early European knowledge about the topography, resources, and waterways of North America. Father Jean de Brébeuf, founder of the Huronia mission, reported that Lake Erie was not a river but a lake. Father Dablon explored the Ottawa River north of Lake Superior and provided extensive information on the upper Great Lakes region. Isaac Jogues and Charles Raymbault became the first white men on record to reach present-day Sault Sainte Marie, and Father Charles Albanel, by all accounts an inveterate explorer, discovered a land and river route to James Bay in 1672, having been commissioned by the colonial authorities to assert France's claim in the area. The following year, Father Jacques Marquette, who succeeded Allouez at the Saint Esprit mission, became the first European, along with the former Jesuit lay brother Louis Jolliet, to reach the upper Mississippi and to confirm, by way of Indian accounts, that the river flowed into the Gulf of Mexico and not, as many hoped, the China seas.

Allouez and other seventeenth-century Jesuit fathers came to North America during the early years of French exploration, when there were still discoveries to be made. They rivaled Étienne

Brulé and the coureurs de bois, the free-spirited young French Canadians who roamed the wilderness with the Indians, adopting native dress and customs and illegally profiting from the fur trade, in moving west of the French Saint Lawrence River valley settlements. Yet unlike the traders, they had usually received a solid education, had often been trained in linguistics, mathematics, geography, or cartography, and left an abundance of written records. They were well equipped, within the intellectual confines of their time, to play the part of scholar and explorer as well as proselytizer. Spreading the faith, moreover, depended on being able to reach and interact successfully with native communities. The detailed reports and summaries of Allouez's and other fathers' ventures, published annually in the *Jesuit Relations,* helped to raise funds for the American mission. Today, they survive as an invaluable record of the continent's human landscape before the onset of large-scale European settlement, providing descriptions of native spiritual beliefs, myths, rituals, artifacts, medical practices, migration patterns, and political, social, and economic systems.

During the pinnacle of its influence in North America, roughly between the mid-1630s and late 1660s, the Jesuit order wielded considerable power and was a leading agent of exploration in New France. Allouez and other early fathers were religiously zealous, fiercely devoted to the spiritual and institutional interests of their order, and determined to maintain a monopoly on the North American mission field. I, for one, am uncomfortable with the assumption that native people needed Christian salvation, be it in seventeenth-century North America or twentieth-century colonial Africa, where my paternal grandparents spent four decades spreading their Lutheran faith. He a minister and she a nurse, my grandparents met as missionaries in the field in their late twenties, a few years after the close of World War I. Working as a team, they founded and staffed a number of remote posts for the Swedish Mission Society, one of several so-called Free Churches that, inspired partly by American revivalism, arose to challenge the state church in the late 1800s.

Not unlike the early Jesuits, my Protestant grandparents traveled widely in areas that had seen no previous European presence. They developed an intimate knowledge of the languages and customs of the fishing and farming communities that lined the Congo River, straddling the colonial divide between France and Belgium. They willingly chose to live and raise children in places that offered little, if any, of the comfort to which European society had accustomed them. Like other Swedish missionaries, they were instructed to write their wills before leaving for Africa, and my grandfather died from malaria, as did many others.

The first Jesuit mission in New France was established in 1610 at Port Royale in Nova Scotia. The mission was destroyed by English Protestant colonists in 1613, and the Jesuits did not resume work in New France until the following decade. In the meantime, in 1615, Samuel de Champlain, who had founded the settlement of Stadacona, present-day Quebec, in 1608, invited the Franciscan Recollét order to begin proselytizing among the surrounding Huron communities. One decade later, Champlain asked the Jesuits to return to North America to work alongside the Recolléts in Huronia.

For Champlain and the Jesuits, religious and political interests in the New World frequently overlapped. Champlain, a devout Catholic, hoped to strengthen French territorial claims by befriending Native American tribes and encouraging them to establish mission-based agricultural villages. Missions, he believed, would advance the spread of Catholicism as well as French political and trade influence and would also attract would-be immigrants from France. The Jesuit order, a powerful political force in Counter-Reformation France, used its authority to exclude competing orders from the mission field and keep non-Catholic settlers from the colony. The fathers supported Champlain's native settlement plans, which they believed would make it easier for them to proselytize, and used their connections with French officials and traders to secure guns, blankets, kettles, beads, axes, and other goods with which to aid and reward their native converts.

Champlain and the Jesuits faced tough challenges, however, in consolidating French control in North America. The immigrant stream from France was small, in part because the persecuted Protestant Huguenots were banned from the colony. The settlers who came preferred trading over farming and partly due to Iroquois hostilities, were reluctant to move beyond the Saint Lawrence River valley. Prospects for increased immigration surfaced in 1627 when the Company of One Hundred Associates brought the first of a promised large wave of new settlers in exchange for having received a monopoly over the colony's fur trade. Plans were quickly dashed when the British occupied Quebec the following year, forcing four hundred settlers to sail back across the Atlantic without ever having set foot on the American continent, with Champlain and the Jesuits in tow.

When the Jesuits returned to New France four years later, they were granted exclusive rights to the missionary field and undertook an ambitious effort to rebuild their mission among the Huron. Yet the colony's prospects languished in the face of royal disinterest, the failure to attract settlers and restore Indian trade networks, and the political void that was left by the death of Champlain in 1636. Before long, the Jesuits faced another challenge to their work, this one in the form of the Iroquois League, which with sympathies among the English and Dutch, attacked and destabilized Huron villages throughout the 1640s. In 1649, the League destroyed Huronia, in the process pillaging missions and killing several fathers and forcing the surviving Huron to disperse. For the Jesuits, the collapse of Huronia provided a harsh lesson in the fragility of their North American labors.

The loss of their Huron stronghold, along with the Iroquois blockade of the Ottawa River, forced the Jesuits to retreat to Quebec. In 1660, after Pierre Radisson and Médard Chouart, sieur des Groseilliers, successfully penetrated the blockade, the fathers turned their attention to the unexplored western hinterland and began to consolidate their influence in the upper Great Lakes region. It was on the brink of these changes that Allouez arrived in New France in 1658. After spending seven years in the Saint Lawrence River valley, he devoted the rest of his thirty-year missionary career to working among the Ottawa, Huron, Illinois, and Miami Indians of the American interior. He founded his first mission on the upper Great Lakes at Saint Esprit, where he arrived on October 1, 1665.

The Jesuit effort to establish a mission on Lake Superior had gotten off to an inauspicious start. Having reached the lake, Radisson and Groseilliers had spent the winter of 1659–60 at Chequamegon Bay, where they encountered friendly bands of Huron and Ottawa. The following spring, Father René Ménard set out to establish a mission at Chequamegon, only to become lost and die in the wilderness after having been abandoned by his Indian guides. The founding of Saint Esprit was thus delayed until Allouez reached the bay in 1665. As his journal describes, Allouez had received an unwelcome introduction to the hardships of wilderness service en route to his destination, having been forced to eat rotten meat and mosses to avoid starvation.

Seeing the increase in French trade activity on Lake Superior after the break in the blockade, Allouez developed ambitious plans for Saint Esprit, which he hoped to develop into a hub for surrounding native communities as well as French traders and prospective settlers. Yet he wanted not only to proselytize and establish a Jesuit and French presence in the area but also to explore Lake Superior and surrounding waterways in hopes of advancing French knowledge of the geography of the American interior. He had arrived at Chequamegon by spending a month paddling the southern shore from Sault Sainte Marie. In May of 1667, he explored the western lake during a nine-day journey from the bay to the Nipigon River, from where he headed north to visit the Nipissing Indians.

By the time Allouez left Chequamegon Bay in 1669, he was far from having sorted out the vexing geography of the American interior. Beyond references to the lake's shape—"almost like that of a bow"—its clear waters, excellent fishing, copper resources, and scattered islands, "The Journal of the Voyage of Father Claude Allouez to the Land of the Outaouacs [Ottawas]" contains only sparse descriptions of the natural features of the Superior region. Some elaboration is provided by Father Dablon in his narrative on the Saint Esprit mission, which was presumably based on Allouez's reports, in the *Jesuit Relations* of 1667–68. Yet missionary labors had left little time for exploration. The already converted Huron, Allouez quickly discovered, had barely sustained their faith, and the pagan Ottawa seemed indifferent and even hostile to the Catholic message. In spite of, or perhaps because of, his missionary zeal, by the time the Ottawa began to show signs of becoming more receptive to conversion, Allouez had grown frustrated with the challenges at Saint Esprit. Barely four years after his arrival, he relocated to Green Bay, where he founded a new mission among the Illinois Indians.

Succeeding Allouez at Saint Esprit was one of the best-known missionaries in North American history, Father Jacques Marquette. Fluent in several Indian languages and having a keen interest in exploration, Marquette hoped to make headway with the Huron and Ottawa as well as explore Lake Superior and surrounding regions. Like Allouez, he had little luck in either while at Chequamegon. Only a year after his arrival, hostilities between the Huron and Ottawa, on the one hand, and the area's Dakota inhabitants, on the other, forced him to abandon Saint Esprit and relocate to Manitoulin Island, in the Straits of Mackinac on western Lake Huron, where he founded the Mission of Saint Ignace. It was from there that he undertook the journey to the upper Mississippi in 1673 by which his place in history was secured.

By then, changing political conditions in the colony were rapidly undermining the Jesuits' ability to explore and proselytize freely in the western hinterland. After decades of struggle, the colony's prospects began to take a turn for the better in the mid-1600s, largely as a result of France's decision to establish a competent royal administration in Quebec. As Jesuit and other emissaries who had repeatedly petitioned the French court to become more assertive in countering English influence and Iroquois hostilities in North America had anticipated, France's about-face paid quick dividends.

With the arrival of a regiment from France, the Iroquois sued for peace in 1666, making the Great Lakes safe for French traders and travelers. To honor the regiment's commander, the Marquis de Tracy, Allouez bestowed on Lake Superior the name of "Lac Tracy"; though short-lived, the name appeared in the *Relations* in the title of Dablon's "Narrative of the Mission of the Holy Ghost among the Outaouacs at Lake Tracy, formerly called Lake Superior," as well as on a few subsequent maps. An able new intendant, Jean-Baptiste Talon, assumed control of the colony's political and economic affairs. Never one to lack for initiative, Talon took measures to revive westward exploration and trade, increase settlement, and expand agriculture, offering free land to immigrants and bringing shiploads of young, unmarried French women to the colony. As the colony and its native allies began to experience a newfound order and security, the fathers were able to proselytize and found missions with an eye to the future.

However, the decades' old void into which the Jesuit order had stepped following Champlain's death was rapidly filling, and with a more assertive colonial policy, growing numbers of French traders and soldiers began to move into the interior. Talon considered Saint Esprit and other missions important in consolidating French power, yet he believed that the Jesuits wielded too much authority, secular as well as religious, within the colony. He sought to distance the fathers from Quebec by removing them from the settler parishes and confining them to the Indian missions. His views were shared by Comte de Frontenac, who arrived as the colony's new governor in 1672. Determined to strengthen France's hold over the interior and viewing the fathers as too tolerant of native ways, Frontenac overrode Jesuit objections and set up new military and trade outposts, as well as invited the less politically ambitious Recollét order to proselytize in the Superior region. Furthermore, men such as Robert Cavalier, sieur de la Salle, who held a long-standing personal grudge against the Catholic fathers, encroached on the Jesuits' role in the field of colonial exploration.

The Jesuits' increasingly tenuous position within the colony was reflected in the debate over the sale of alcohol to the Indians. The Jesuits argued that alcohol, which was usually given to native suppliers on credit in exchange for future furs, was destroying the social fabric of Indian communities and enabling traders to exploit and underpay their suppliers. Their position was supported by Quebec's first bishop, François-Xavier de Laval, who had arrived in 1659, and in addition to condemning what he saw as the frivolous lifestyle of many French settlers, favored excommunicating anyone who sold alcohol to the Indians. Yet although Laval had studied under the Jesuits and shared many of their convictions, he was not a member of the order and, at the Pope's request, reported directly to Rome, not to the French Catholic church. In petitioning the French court to ban alcohol from the American interior, the Jesuits found themselves at loggerheads with civil authorities and settlers in the colony who believed that the brandy trade helped to maintain France's native alliances and supply networks and to discourage the Indians from taking their furs to British traders.

The fathers' motives in opposing the brandy trade had already come under scrutiny in Allouez's days. Accounts indicate that the Jesuits had a significant stake in the fur trade. Whether the fathers traded in pelts primarily to obtain supplies for their missions and knives, blankets, kettles, and other goods for their converts or to enrich the order, and even themselves, has been the subject of debate. Yet to the extent that they profited or benefited from the fur trade, it has been suggested that their efforts to restrict brandy, as well as illegal traders, from Indian country was motivated not mainly by a desire to protect native communities from vice and exploitation but, rather, to preserve their own supply networks and reduce competition from other traders.

Wherever the truth may lie and however bitterly the fathers complained about the deceit, drunkenness, and promiscuity of traders in the interior, the availability of French goods served, to varying degrees, as an inducement for Indians to visit the missions. Native communities that had early access to French goods also often profited by serving as middlemen between French traders and more distant tribes. Concerning the spread of French influence, moreover, the activities of missionaries and traders tended to be mutually reinforcing. Through their travels, both expanded French knowledge of the geography and resources of the American hinterland. Through their relations with native communities, both provided a foundation of contacts upon which others later built. Trade and mission outposts encouraged the Indians to center their material well-being and cultural frameworks around those of colonial society. Meanwhile, the spread of French firearms, which required a continuous supply of spare parts and powder to operate, increasingly compelled Native Americans to link their security to the colony's fortunes.

As the colony reached new political and economic heights during the latter decades of the 1600s, the influence of the Jesuits continued to decline. Growing tensions between France and England furthered a centralization of power and a mounting military presence throughout the colony. The Jesuits lost many of their lay functions as well as their freedom to travel and to choose locations for their missions at will. At the same time, growing royal absolutism and a decline in religious fervor in France weakened the order and reduced the availability of funds and qualified recruits for missionary endeavors. New recruits, who often came from the lower classes, lacked the intellectual curiosity, the missionary zeal, and the thirst for adventure that had induced Allouez and other early fathers to welcome the challenges of wilderness service in the American interior. Before long, the Jesuits had begun to close missions and to concentrate their western operations around the Saint Ignace mission and the trade post at Mackinac.

Jacques Marquette's departure from Saint Esprit for Mackinac marked the end of Jesuit missionary work at Chequamegon Bay. The bay saw little other French activity until 1693, when in keeping with the times, Pierre Le Sueur arrived with a contingent of traders and soldiers. While priests occasionally visited Grand Portage, Sault Sainte Marie, and possibly other locations around the lake, the Catholic missionary presence on Superior was not reestablished until 1835, when the famous Austrian-born Slovene father Frederic Baraga came to Chequamegon. By the time Baraga arrived on the lake, the Ojibwe had largely supplanted the Dakota on the southern and western shores, and the Superior region had passed from the French to the English, who confiscated abandoned Jesuit properties, and ultimately to the Americans. Trade and other activity in the Chequamegon area had shifted from the mainland, where Allouez had established his mission, to the village of La Pointe, named after the original mission of La Pointe du Saint Esprit, on nearby Madeline Island. Moreover, Baraga's arrival at La Pointe was largely a response to the opening in 1834 of a mission on the island by the Protestant Reverend Sherman Hall.

Baraga, who spent over three decades ministering to native and settler communities around Lake Superior, is one of the few latter-day Catholic fathers to have equaled, if not surpassed, the early Jesuits in the extent of his travels and the depth and import of his understanding of Indian languages and customs. He wrote several popular works on native culture and apart from his legendary winter journeys by snowshoe and dogsled between his five Lake Superior missions, he is probably best known for having produced the first dictionary and grammar of the Ojibwe language, published in 1850. Baraga had been trained as a linguist, spoke a handful of European languages, and before coming to the Superior region, had served among the Ottawa, a related Algonquin-speaking people, for whom he had translated prayer books and religious texts.

Missionaries, who needed to be able to converse with their converts, were often the first Europeans to produce lexicons, grammars, and related works for native languages; Baraga wrote his dictionary and grammar mainly to help other missionaries learn Ojibwe. The best of these missionary works survive as an invaluable historical record of native languages as they were spoken before the spread of English and French. The Recollét brother Gabriel Sagard's lexicon and phrase book from 1624 provides one of the few surviving records of the original Huron language, much of which was lost following the tribe's 1649 dispersal. Baraga's considerably more comprehensive dictionary and grammar, written over a century and a half ago, continues to offer one of the best available sources for recovering no-longer-spoken words in the Ojibwe language.

Allouez, Baraga, and other Catholic fathers made far-reaching contributions to Western knowledge of the landscape and native communities of the Lake Superior region. Their contributions re-quired patient observation, intellectual flexibility, sensitivity, and respect. The writings of Allouez and Baraga, as well as a host of seventeenth-century fathers such as Lalemant, François du Peron, and Francesco-Giuseppe Bressani, reveal a profound admiration for the self-sufficiency, skill, social cohesion, and other virtues that had enabled Native Americans to survive in the harsh and trying natural environment of the American wilderness. These same writings, however, also refer to the Indians as savages and remark disparagingly on their beliefs and personal habits.

As their familiarity with native society gradually increased, early Jesuit fathers generally became more tolerant of Indian ways and customs and attempted to adapt their message to the cultural frameworks they encountered. Unlike later Protestant missionar-ies, they saw conversion as the beginning, not the culmination, of the individual's commitment to a Christian lifestyle. While their respect for native ways may have fallen far short of that of the coureurs de bois, they shied away from making cultural as-similation a prerequisite for baptism; later Catholic missionaries, including Baraga, did not always retain the early Jesuits' tolerance. With little success in settling the land and only marginal interest in assimilation, the seventeenth-century French tended, on the whole, to be less disruptive in their impact on native society than were the English and, later, the Americans. Not surprisingly perhaps, while the Jesuits performed an impressive number of baptisms, most of their converts failed to sustain or pass on their faith.

In a way, I cannot help but admire Allouez and other fathers who willingly spent years and even decades in remote places that, save for traders and explorers, few white men crossed, let alone lived in. Regardless of their motives and the wider power structures to which they belonged, they endured considerable personal hardship and isolation and, as Ménard's fate reveals, not infrequently found themselves at the mercy of their Indian guides. Driven by an unshakable faith and confidence, they were convinced that Christianity would benefit the people among whom they served. So too were my grandparents. Such a conviction may seem paternalistic or at least misguided to many today, but for centuries, it was commonplace across much of the Western world.

Looking back on the Jesuits' movement across the American interior, I find it heartening to know that many of the early fathers who came to Lake Superior owe their place in the history books to their contributions as scholars and explorers, not only as proselytizers. The wide range of their activities and concerns, it seems to me, provides for a more interesting, if still controversial, legacy than anything conversion alone could have accomplished.

Gathering Instincts

GATHERING IS DEEP-SEATED IN THE HUMAN PSYCHE.
Human survival no longer depends on foraging for bulbs, berries,
and other edibles. Yet instincts tend to linger long after their evolutionary purpose has been served, and the urge to gather, to wander and fill our hands with the shapes and textures of the natural
world, persists. During years of coastal living, pearly white shells
had beckoned me like beacons on the damp tidal sands. When
Lake Superior's shore offered few comparable summons, I quickly
fell out of the gathering habit. Yet instincts have a way of creeping up on us. Walking on the shore a few summers ago, I pressed
a purple flower from a small, unusual-looking plant between the
pages of my notebook. The flower, I later discovered, belonged to
a butterwort plant, a carnivorous arctic-range species that can be
found in isolated moist pockets on the lakeshore. This casual kind
of gathering quickly became a habit. I have yet to preserve a specimen beyond what is needed to learn its name. But I think I have
begun to understand the hard yet gratifying work and the deeply
personal bond with the natural world that gathering brings.

Quite by chance, browsing the shelves of the local public library, I recently came across a few books on the lives of early American women naturalists, many of whom became experts on plants not well known in their day. These pioneering women mounted, organized, and cataloged their growing specimen collections with great care and dedication and, I cannot help but think, would have frowned on the casual kind of gathering I do. For the most part, they lived on the East and West Coasts, yet a few studied plants in northern regions. All were remarkable for their time in that with or without the support of those around them, they bucked traditional roles and successfully structured their lives around a determined, if often solitary and challenging, quest to explore America's natural landscape.

Among these women were Jane Colden, who collected and illustrated plants in mid-eighteenth-century New York; Agnes Chase, who collected over ten thousand specimens of grasses from across the country; and Annie Alexander and Louise Kellogg, who together gathered plants, fossils, shells, and small mammals and discovered several new species of grasses in the deserts and mountains of the Southwest. Alice Eastwood gathered wildflowers and native plants in the Colorado Rockies and on the California coast; Kate Furbish collected, classified, and illustrated many of the plants of Maine; and Elizabeth Gertrude Knight Britton, probably the most prominent turn-of-the-century female botanist, was an expert on mosses and ferns. Mary Treat, an amateur botanist who worked in the New Jersey pine barrens, studied butterworts, sundews, pitcher plants, bladderworts, and other carnivorous plants, many of which can also be found in the bogs around Lake Superior.

Among those who gathered in northern regions, Eloise Butler, a native of Maine who came to Minnesota as a teacher in 1874, became a pioneer in the effort to preserve and restore America's native plant communities. In 1907, she established the wildflower garden that bears her name in Minneapolis's Theodore Wirth Park, the first garden in the country devoted entirely to native species.

Butler, who was largely self-taught, also collected specimens from local bogs and discovered several new species and new varieties of already familiar species of microscopic freshwater algae.

Belonging to a slightly later generation was Olga Lakela, who had emigrated to Minnesota from Finland as a child. Lakela, a professor of biology at the University of Minnesota-Duluth, published over seventy-five books and articles on the plant and bird life of Minnesota, Lake Superior, and the northern forest region. Her life's work, *A Flora of Northeastern Minnesota,* describes more than thirteen hundred species from Saint Louis and Lake Counties. In the mid-1940s, Lakela made several trips to study the unspoiled vegetation of Lake Superior's Beaver Island; she later petitioned the Reserve Mining Company to reconsider plans to quarry the island's rock to build a breakwater. She also started and contributed an estimated thirty thousand specimens to the herbarium that bears her name at the University of Minnesota-Duluth.

In addition to botanists and naturalists, there were also women floral illustrators. Illustration, however, had its roots in Victorian England and was a much more acceptable—and in many circles a quite fashionable—female pursuit. Jean Jacques Rousseau published *Letters on the Elements of Botany, Addressed to a Lady* in 1785, and subsequent decades witnessed a proliferation of flower painting how-to books directed mainly at women. While in scientific circles botanical drawing was often looked upon as little more than a pastime, a number of female illustrators produced works of considerable accuracy and sensitivity.

Clarissa W. Munger Badger's book of hand-colored *Floral Belles from the Green-house and Garden,* published in 1867, was widely imitated by men and women illustrators alike. Closer to home, Maine native Emily Hitchcock Terry's collection of watercolors, *American Flowers,* drew heavily on paintings from the twelve years she spent living with her ailing husband in Minnesota. Exquisite representation, moreover, was not only for the illustrators. Recognized botanical experts, such as Agnes

Chase and Kate Furbish, also made drawings and paintings of their specimens or illustrated the works of colleagues.

Early women botanists were a varied bunch. Some, such as Britton, Lakela, and Kate Brandegee, had formal educations. Many more, including Butler, Chase, Eastwood, and Treat, were largely self-taught or, as Colden was, educated by their fathers. Most were married, and of these, some, such as Colden, collected and classified only during their single years. Others, including Furbish and Eastwood, never married. Some gathered alone, and others, such as Britton and Brandegee, with husbands, friends, or fathers. As a group, women botanists were disproportionately represented among amateur ranks. Many fewer female than male botanists had formal scientific training, published books and articles, became museum curators, or held academic and professional affiliations. Britton, who authored more than three hundred scientific papers and eventually became honorary curator of mosses at the New York Botanical Garden, was, perhaps tellingly, the only female charter member of the American Botanical Society.

The contributions of amateur naturalists, however, did not always go unrecognized. Several female amateurs corresponded with Charles Darwin, Asa Gray, and other leading male scientists, who credited them in publications and named species after them. Moreover, some women attained prestigious positions, despite being largely self-taught. Such was the case with Alice Eastwood, who became curator of botany at the California Academy of Sciences upon the retirement of her mentor, Kate Brandegee, and her husband in 1892. By the time Eastwood herself retired at the age of ninety over half a century later, she had added 340,000 specimens to the academy's herbarium and published about three hundred papers. In recognition of her significant contributions, she was invited to serve as honorary president of the Eighth International Botanical Congress in Stockholm in 1950.

Agnes Chase, another largely self-taught botanist, worked for the U.S. Department of Agriculture's Bureau of Plant Industry, in addition to publishing over seventy papers and articles and being active in the suffragist, prohibitionist, and socialist movements. And after her marriage ended in the 1870s, Mary Treat successfully supported herself with royalties from her popular 1880 book *Home Studies in Nature* and other publications.

The motivations of early women botanists were as varied as their backgrounds. Some were drawn to the natural world by long-standing scientific interests, others by chance encounters with an intriguing species. Some sought to experience in nature the beauty of God's creation, others only to find solitude and independence. Reflecting on their lives, I cannot help but think that the latter motivation must have entered prominently into their gathering pursuits. This was probably especially true of those who married and had children, many of whom seemed to lead two different lives—the one grounded in the child-rearing and homemaking tasks that society and their own socialization had put forth as proper female pursuits, the other in the wilderness forays and specimen classifying or illustrating that must have brought them an otherwise unattainable level of personal freedom and satisfaction.

Whatever their motivations, the lives of these pioneering women revolved around an intimate connection with the objects of the natural world. For them, the urge to gather seemed instinctual, as natural and compelling as if it had been passed down from generations of mothers and grandmothers to sisters and daughters. In some ways it had. Women were the primary gatherers of plants and edibles, men the primary hunters and fishers, in most foraging societies. Once settled life emerged, women continued to be intimately involved in procuring nature's bounty, growing crops and tending gardens of edibles and remedies. Such activities carried into colonial America.

Today, gathering is a pastime to be indulged, not the carefully honed survival skill it once was. It may lie dormant for years, or even decades, only to be reawakened by the smallest of inducements. It is, I have also found, a rather habit-forming act. One kind of gathering quickly leads to another, and the summer after

I began to take specimens of shrubs and flowers, I started to notice the rich assortment of pebbles on the shore. I recently filled a small wicker basket with my first collection, gathered over the course of several years. I saw this as a minor feat, indicative of a maturation of my gathering habits. I have yet to press and mount a leaf or flower, but I think I am finally beginning to understand the satisfaction that early women naturalists derived from adding to and organizing and displaying their growing specimen collections. How these collections must, for many of them, have served not only as scientific representations of flora but as cumulative memories of long, satisfying days spent gathering in the field.

It is this same yearning to feel that even though our lives no longer revolve around foraging, we can still pick and touch and be enriched by nature's bounty that moves people to head for the woods in search of berries, to the beach in search of shells or pebbles, or to any other place where there are edibles or mementos to be found. Deep in the subconscious of this longing, I believe, lies a desire to feel the continuity that ties one life to another—that places me in a long line of women gatherers who have found in their natural surroundings the axis around which to locate their lives.

The Brule River

AT THE END OF THE BRULE RIVER ROAD, A FEW MILES off Highway 13 in northwestern Wisconsin, a large dirt parking lot gives way to a grassy picnic area overlooking the lakeshore. A short dusty road leads down to the mouth of the Brule River. An old station wagon has been backed down the road, and a family of five is fishing at the river's mouth. The scenic, trout-filled waters of the Brule have been drawing anglers, including the likes of Presidents Grant, Cleveland, Coolidge, Hoover, and Eisenhower, for the past century and a half. Today, these waters are protected within the border of the Brule River State Forest. Before anglers and other recreational visitors discovered the Brule, a steady stream of famous explorers, from Pierre Le Sueur and Jonathan Carver to Lewis Cass and Henry Schoolcraft, came and went at the river's mouth, as did countless traders, loggers, and other men whose names escaped the historical record. As I look out at the long slender beach that lines the shore, the station wagon fades from view. Just as the imprints of my steps vanish in the waterlogged sands, so too the mouth of the Brule bears few visible reminders of the triumphs and disappointments its waters once spawned.

The river's clear, spring-fed waters descend four hundred feet during their forty-odd-mile run north toward Lake Superior. The lands that surround the upper and lower river comprise two distinct ecological regions. The inland portions of the state forest are characterized mainly by sandy soils and pine barrens, while impermeable clays and aspen, spruce, and fir forests dominate the areas around the lower river. Underlying the Brule landscape is a thick sequence of sandstone, extending southwest from the Bayfield Peninsula toward the regions of the lower Saint Louis River in Minnesota. Inland of the sandstone, at the southern edge of the state forest, a terminal moraine of the Superior ice lobe provides the rich, deep soils favored by northern hardwoods.

Different natural environments have produced variations in the river's channel and flow. While the upper Brule River is calm and slow-moving, the lower Brule sets a more spirited course over sandstone ledges, its currents fed by runoff from the erosion-prone clays that once formed the bottom of Glacial Lake Duluth. Before European settlers arrived, the clay plain along the lower Brule held Wisconsin's largest boreal forest, with ample stands of birch and white pine, a few large specimens of which still remain. As elsewhere, turn-of-the-century land clearing for logging and agriculture and postlogging fires removed trees and other soil-binding vegetation throughout the watershed. Extensive replant-ing of jack and red pine has taken place along the upper river, yet the lower clay plain remains especially vulnerable to erosion. In late spring, a large fan of silt-laden water, its color somewhere between mellow rust and deep auburn, extends into the lake, its sands feeding the long beach that lines the river's bank.

A large wooden sign in the picnic area, which provides an overview of the river's history, credits Daniel Greysolon, sieur Du Luth, with being the first white man to enter the Brule in 1680. Following a Native American water route, Du Luth charted an inland course for European traders and explorers, portaging from the Brule to Lake Saint Croix and the Saint Croix River, from where he continued on to the Mississippi. The wooden sign does not mention the origin of the river's name, which is apparently in some doubt. Not unlike that of the Gooseberry River, which enters the lake on the Minnesota shore, the name of the Brule may be a reference to a French explorer, but in translation also has a French as well as an Ojibwe meaning. Étienne Brulé left no written chronicles of his journeys, and while it presently seems unlikely that he ventured as far west as the Brule, he has often been credited with being the first white man to reach Lake Superior, as well as Lakes Huron, Erie, and Ontario, and to paddle down the Ottawa River, thus opening up a water route that allowed the French to reach Superior by way of two lesser rivers and Lakes Nipissing and Huron. Médard Chouart, sieur des Groseilliers, whose surname translates to "of the Gooseberries," apparently lost his notes during his return trip from the lake in 1659–60. It is not known for certain, therefore, whether he camped at the mouth of the Gooseberry River, which may have been named after him, if its name did not derive from an Ojibwe phrase of the same meaning.

As far as Étienne Brulé and the Brule are concerned, Brulé worked as a scout and interpreter for Samuel Champlain, whose service he entered in 1608 at the age of sixteen. One year later, he spent the winter among the Huron, thus becoming the first white man to learn the Indians' language and customs. Expanding the fur trade depended on establishing friendly relations with native communities, as did learning about the water routes, trade networks, and mineral resources of the American interior. A geographer by training, Champlain had a penchant for exploration, hoping to discover a water passage to Asia. As the fledgling French colony demanded more of his attention, he relied on Brulé and other young agents, along with their Huron guides, to explore on his behalf.

In 1632, Champlain published a map of New France on which he included a large western lake. Assuming that the lake was

Superior, a number of later historical accounts maintained that Champlain's depiction must have been based on descriptions provided by Brulé, an interpretation that was further supported by the claim made in a 1636 book by the Franciscan Recollét brother Gabriel Sagard to have been informed by Brulé of a large body of water where copper was mined to the west of Huronia. Brulé, it was surmised, had probably reached Lake Superior sometime between 1615 and 1623. Several scholars, however, have challenged Sagard's account of his meeting with Brulé and have also noted that Champlain's 1632 cartographical depiction could have been based on information received from the Indians and may, moreover, have been of Lake Michigan, not Superior.

Regardless of the extent of his westward explorations, what little is known of Brulé's life makes for a fascinating story. Fearless and adventuresome, the young explorer took to wilderness life with gusto and has been called the first coureur de bois, or "runner of the woods." Many French Canadians frowned at the young man's lifestyle, which in the eyes of Champlain and the Jesuits set a poor example of Christian morals for would-be native converts. Writing in the 1636 *Jesuit Relations,* the founder of the Huronia mission, Father Jean Brébeuf, characterized Brulé's lifestyle as scandalous. Brulé's loyalties to France seem, in any event, to have been rather precarious. In 1628, he helped guide the English, who were at war with France in Europe and had intercepted a French convoy, up the Saint Lawrence River to Quebec. Unable to resupply his colony, Champlain was forced to surrender and retreat to France for three years. Whether over the betrayal of Champlain or an unrelated squabble, Brulé was killed and reportedly eaten by the Huron in 1633, at the age of forty-one.

The sign in the picnic area refers to the river by its full name, the *Bois Brulé,* a name that reportedly came from the French translation of Ojibwe and Dakota references to the "half burnt wood" river. Early travelers frequently used approximations or translations of native names in referring to new places or natural features they encountered. In the journal of his 1767 expedition, colonial

explorer Jonathan Carver refers to the Brule as the *Nacisaquoit.*
Charles Trowbridge, who partook in Michigan Governor Lewis
Cass's 1820 expedition along Lake Superior's southern shore,
called the river *"La Riviere Broulé,* or Burnt River," as did Colonel
Thomas McKenney, head of the Bureau of Indian Affairs, who
led an expedition from Sault Sainte Marie to Fond du Lac and
used the spelling Brulé in his 1827 *Sketches of a Tour to the Lakes.*
And the French geographer and explorer Joseph Nicollet includes
both the Ojibwe name *Wissakude* and the English translation
Burnt Wood River on his 1843 map of the upper Mississippi area.

The source of the Ojibwe name for the Brule is usually explained with reference to the fires that swept through the pine
forests that line the upper river. Before European settlement,
fires were started by lightning strikes and possibly also by native
peoples, who in many parts of North America used low-intensity
burns to clear land, renew berry patches, attract wildlife, drive
game, and improve visibility for hunting and defense. In the
southern Lake Superior region, Dakota and Ojibwe communities may have used fire to maintain habitats that maximized
the growth of blueberries and attracted deer, grouse, and other
game that prefer to browse on saplings and regrowth vegetation.
Given relatively sparse population densities, however, it is unclear
whether human-initiated fires would have been frequent enough
to have had a significant environmental impact. Yet whether
started by humans or nature, regularly occurring burns favored
the spread of species, such as pines, that could survive surface
flames and regenerate quickly in postfire soils.

With its lowlands rich in berries, game, and wild rice, the
upper Brule and Saint Croix River valleys supported a variegated
native economy. By the time Du Luth arrived at the Brule, the
Ojibwe were gradually moving westward along the southern lakeshore, encroaching on traditional Dakota grounds. To make the
area safe for European travel, Du Luth negotiated a truce between
the warring tribes. Within a few decades, however, the region
entered a long period of intermittent warfare, toward the end of

which, in 1842, according to an official Wisconsin highway marker, the Ojibwe defeated a much larger Dakota force in a major battle on the upper Brule. With growing European settlement, the fruits of victory would have been short-lived for either nation.

Northwestern Wisconsin's river is not the only place that bears the name *Brule* around Lake Superior. Minnesota's Brule River, which descends to the lake through Judge C. R. Magney State Park, is identified as the *Wisacodé* on a mid-nineteenth-century state geological survey map, indicating that it too probably derived its name from the Ojibwe translation. Another Brule River enters the lake along the Michigan-Wisconsin border, and there is also a Brulé Harbor and a Brule Point on the Ontario coastline. Places called *Brule,* moreover, can be found in Canada and the United States where neither Étienne Brulé nor the Ojibwe ever ventured, but where there was a French presence. This suggests that in the different locations where it appears, the name probably did not come from the same source. In many places, the French word for "burnt," *brulé,* in either its original or anglicized form, may simply have been a convenient way for early travelers to refer to areas that had been scarred by fire. In others, the name may have originated with translations from the Ojibwe, or may even be associated with the legacy of Étienne Brulé. The uncertain origin of place-names seems a fitting legacy for the complex, centuries-old interaction of native and French, to which belonged a continuous flow not only of trade but also of idioms and ideas around Lake Superior's shores.

Unbeknownst to them, native and early French traders who used the Brule–Saint Croix passage were following a path cut 10,000 years ago, when the two vastly swollen rivers served as the only outlet for glacial meltwaters from the Superior basin. Until around 9,500 years ago, by which time enough ice had melted to the east to allow drainage toward the Atlantic via the Great Lakes basin, meltwaters flowed through the Brule and Saint Croix toward the Mississippi River and the Gulf of Mexico. As the glacial waters receded, the two rivers were eventually separated by a hill that became the north-south continental divide, and the Brule reversed its course. Their headwaters lie only half a mile apart and for early travelers, the two-mile portage between the Brule and Lake Saint Croix was an easy walk.

The lower Brule, however, was apparently not an easy paddle. Boulders frequently tore holes in the canoes, and cargo had to be hauled around rapids and ledges. Du Luth noted in his journal that he had to remove a hundred beaver dams before he was able to paddle up the river. Using the Brule to return to Lake Superior after his 1832 discovery of the source of the Mississippi, Schoolcraft complained of the many repairs that had to be made to his canoes. I can imagine the relief of men traveling up the river upon reaching the quiet, boggy waters above Lenroot Falls. As is the case along the upper Brule, bogs often occupy poorly drained, postglacial lake beds. Since few trees can tolerate the cold, nutrient-poor growing environment, the bog forest is dominated by black spruce, tamarack, and white cedar, the latter usually concentrated in swamps. Loggers who moved into the Brule watershed in the late nineteenth century left the bog forest largely untouched. Today, it probably forms the only area along the river's course that looks much as it did when the first white explorers arrived.

Not long after the era of exploration had run its course around the lake, European settlers began moving into the Brule watershed. As the wooden sign in the picnic area indicates, in 1839 the American Fur Company established a fish camp on the river. In the 1840s, prospectors unsuccessfully explored for copper in the area, and in the early 1870s, a brief mining venture was attempted. The river also became the site of a short-lived socialist experiment when a man by the name of Samuel Blodgett purchased the Percival mine and a few thousand acres around the lakeshore and convinced a group of fellow Bristolites to try their hands at cooperative farming, fishing, and barrel-making in the newly founded village of Clevedon. The village apparently had all the makings of success, including plenty of investment capital, but lacked the human ingenuity and hard work required to survive on the harsh shores of Lake Superior. Within five years, it had failed, and its residents returned to England.

Having not taken to logging, Clevedon residents reportedly bought wood from nearby sawmills. Cutting their way through the forests around the Brule, late-nineteenth-century loggers built a log dam half a mile upstream and sorted wood at the river's mouth. Fortunately, a more serious challenge to the river's flow never came to pass. In the mid-1890s, the Brule–Saint Croix route was surveyed at congressional request, along with the Saint Louis River–Savannah portage west of Duluth, as part of a proposal to construct a barge channel, replete with locks and dams, between Lake Superior and the Mississippi. The roughly 200-mile pro-posed Brule–Saint Croix canal was found to be the cheaper of the two routes, but the project never got beyond the planning stages. In 1907, the Frederick Weyerhaeuser Lumber Company donated its land holdings around the Brule, providing the seedbed for the establishment of the state forest that bears the river's name, on the condition that the waters remain unharnessed into the future.

The forty-thousand-acre state forest runs the length of the river but protects only a narrow strip of land. The Brule water-shed, in contrast, covers approximately 180 square miles and includes over seventy streams and smaller tributaries as well as numerous lakes. Lying largely outside the boundaries of the state forest, the watershed is subject to the environmental effects of commercial development and agriculture. Meanwhile, manage-ment plans for the state lands strive to maintain a balance be-tween sustainable timber harvests and recreational use on the one hand, both of which are important for the region's economy, and preserving water quality and natural habitats for rare plant and animal communities, on the other.

A slender stretch of largely undeveloped beach extends west of the river, while just east of the mouth, a small dune covered with wild rose, alder, and red-osier dogwood shrubs borders the lake. Around Lake Superior, sandy beaches and dune environments, which are relatively scarce, are concentrated mainly in Wisconsin and Michigan, whose sedimentary deposits are more easily eroded than the lava-born bedrock of Minnesota. Beaches provide important habitat for endangered plants such as the pitcher's thistle and the Lake Huron tansy, both of which exist only in the Great Lakes region, as well as for migratory birds. Among the latter is the piping plover, a small, sandy-colored bird with orange legs, a black neck band, and a distinctive "peep-lo" whistle, which feeds along estuaries and beaches, where it runs and pecks muds and sands for crustaceans, worms, and insects. Three distinct breeding populations of piping plovers have been identified in the United States. Two of these, on the northern Great Plains and the Atlantic coast, include about thirteen hundred pairs each and are considered threatened but not yet endangered. The third population, which winters along the Gulf Coast, nests on the Great Lakes, and by the time it was listed under the Endangered Species Act in 1985, its numbers had declined from an estimated four to five hundred in presettlement days to only seventeen breeding pairs, all of which were nesting in northern Michigan, most on the eastern Upper Peninsula.

While turn-of-the-century hunting initially decimated its numbers, the piping plover, like the ring-billed gull, staged a recovery after receiving protection under the 1916 U.S.–Canada Migratory Bird Treaty. Today, its survival is threatened mainly by habitat destruction. Piping plovers prefer fairly wide and sparsely vegetated dunes and sand or pebble beaches or mudflats, where they lay three or four speckled eggs in the open sand, their nests often sheltered only by a cobble, a few strands of vegetation, or a piece of driftwood. As industrial and tourist development has increased along Lake Superior's southern shore, undisturbed beach habitat has diminished. As is the case at the mouth of the Brule, fishing, boating, and other forms of recreation are bringing growing numbers of people to the shore.

People and their pets disrupt the piping plover's nesting sites, accidentally stepping on eggs as well as on the tiny, tan chicks that leave the nest within a day of hatching and scurry around the sand flightless for their first three to four weeks of life. The construction of lakeside resorts, vacation homes, and marinas further fragments shore habitat, and by increasing garbage and food scraps, also attracts gulls, raccoons, and other predators that prey on the defenseless chicks. The piping plover's Great Lakes breeding grounds are threatened not only by human activity but also by natural erosion brought on by storm surges and periodically high lake water levels, which inundate beaches.

Intense efforts to protect beach habitat, establish nesting enclosures, and rear chicks in captivity appear to be gradually paying off, and have been aided by recent low lake levels, especially compared to the high waters of the mid-1980s. In 2001, census takers located 32 breeding pairs of piping plovers on the American Great Lakes; the species had also extended its range from Michigan to Wisconsin. This is still a far cry from the 150 breeding pairs called for under the current U.S. Fish and Wildlife Service's recovery plan. The plan designates thirty-five critical habitat areas to be managed for their potential to support future nesting populations along the Great Lakes. Three of these, Michigan's Chequamegon Point and the Saint Louis estuary and Wisconsin Point in the Duluth-Superior harbor area, are on the Superior shore.

Perhaps, some day, piping plovers will extend their nesting range to the beach and small dune around the mouth of the Brule River. Looking past the family of five at the river's mouth, thinking how the steps of famous travelers and explorers and of more ordinary men who chased their dreams up and down the Brule have vanished long ago, I can imagine standing alone one day on yet another waterlogged spit, my soles sinking slowly into the sands, watching for chicks to come scurrying across the shore.

References

IN ADDITION TO THESE BIBLIOGRAPHIC REFERENCES, this work relies on documents, reports, and other primary source materials available through state and county historical societies and departments of natural resources as well as on information from the official Web sites of federal, state, and local agencies, environmental organizations, and citizens' associations.

Agassiz, G. R., ed. *Letters and Recollections of Alexander Agassiz.* Boston and New York: Houghton Mifflin Co., 1913.

Agassiz, Louis. *Lake Superior.* 1850. Reprint, New York: Arno and New York Times, 1970.

Ahlgren, Clifford, and Isabel Ahlgren. *Lob Trees in the Wilderness: The Human and Natural History of the Boundary Waters.* Minneapolis: University of Minnesota Press, 1984.

Aveni, Anthony F. *Native American Astronomy.* Austin: University of Texas Press, 1977.

Bailey, Martha J. *American Women in Science: A Biographical Dictionary.* Santa Barbara, Calif.: ABC-CLIO, 1994.

Barry, James P. *Old Forts of the Great Lakes: Sentinels in the Wilderness.* Lansing, Mich.: Thunder Bay Press, 1994.

Beck, Bill. *Northern Lights: An Illustrated History of Minnesota Power.* Eden Prairie, Minn.: Viking Press, 1986.

Bent, Arthur C. *Life Histories of North American Gulls and Terns.* Washington, D.C.: Government Printing Office, 1921.

Bishop, Hugh E. *By Water and Rail: A History of Lake County, Minnesota.* Duluth, Minn.: Lake Superior Port Cities, 2000.

Blegen, Theodore C. *Minnesota: A History of the State.* 1963. Reprint, Minneapolis: University of Minnesota Press, 1975.

Blunt, Wilfrid. *The Compleat Naturalist: A Life of Linnaeus.* New York: Viking Press, 1971.

Bogue, Margaret Beattie, and Virginia A. Palmer. *Around the Shores of Lake Superior: A Guide to Historic Sites.* Madison: University of Wisconsin Sea Grant College Program, 1979.

Bohm, Robert T. "The Ring-bills Come Back." *Minnesota Conservation Volunteer* 45, 260 (January/February 1982).

Butterfield, Consul Willshire. *History of Brulé's Discoveries and Explorations, 1610–1626.* Cleveland: Helman-Taylor Co., 1898.

Cannon, W. F., et al. *Geologic Map of the Ontonagon and Part of the Wakefield 30' x 60' Quadrangles, Michigan.* Miscellaneous Investigations Series Map I-2499. U.S. Geological Survey, 1995.

Champlain, Samuel. *Voyages to New France.* Trans. Michael Macklem. Ottawa: Oberon Press, 1970.

Charles, Craig. *Exploring Superior Country: The Nature Guide to Lake Superior.* Minocqua, Wis.: North Word Press, 1992.

Clark, James I. *Father Claude Allouez, Missionary.* Madison: State Historical Society of Wisconsin, 1957.

Conway, Thor. *Painted Dreams: Native American Rock Art.* Minocqua, Wis.: North Word Press, 1993.

Cranston, James Herbert. *Étienne Brûlé: Immortal Scoundrel.* Toronto: Ryerson Press, 1949.

Crosby, George H., and Chas. S. Roulo. *Crosby: The Metropolis of the Cuyuna Range.* N.p., [1913?].

Crouse, Nellis M. *Contributions of the Canadian Jesuits to the Geographical Knowledge of New France, 1632–1675.* Ph.D. diss., Cornell University, 1924.

Culkin, William E. *North Shore Place Names.* St. Paul, Minn.: Scott-Mitchell Publishing Co., 1931.

Daniel, Glenda, and Jerry Sullivan. *A Sierra Club Naturalist's Guide: The North Woods of Michigan, Wisconsin, Minnesota, and Southern Ontario.* San Francisco: Sierra Club Books, 1981.

Danziger, Edmund J. *The Chippewas of Lake Superior.* Norman: University of Oklahoma Press, 1978.

Densmore, Frances. *Dakota and Ojibwe People in Minnesota.* St. Paul: Minnesota Historical Society, 1977.

Dewdney, Selwyn. *The Sacred Scrolls of the Southern Ojibway.* Toronto: University of Toronto Press, 1975.

Dewdney, Selwyn, and Kenneth E. Kidd. *Indian Rock Paintings of the Great Lakes.* 1962. Reprint, Toronto: University of Toronto Press, 1973.

Evans, Howard Ensign. *Pioneer Naturalists: The Discovery and Naming of North American Plants and Animals.* New York: Henry Holt and Company, 1993.

Flenley, Ralph. *Samuel de Champlain: Founder of New France.* Toronto: Macmillan Co. of Canada, 1924.

Folwell, William W. *A History of Minnesota.* St. Paul: Minnesota Historical Society, 1922–1930.

Fox, Philip Marvin. *The Link between Three Hundred Years of Travel: The Brule–St. Croix Passage.* Master's thesis, University of Minnesota-Duluth, 1968.

Frängsmyr, Tore, ed. *Linnaeus: The Man and His Work.* Berkeley: University of California Press, 1983.

Frelich, Lee, and Don Carlton. *Ecological and Fire Conditions for the Boundary Waters Canoe Area Wilderness.* Foster Wheeler Environmental Corporation Report, April 2000. USDA Forest Service, Superior National Forest.

Fritzen, John. *The History of Fond du Lac and Jay Cooke Park.* Duluth, Minn.: St. Louis County Historical Society, 1978.

Furtman, Michael. *Magic on the Rocks: Canoe Country Pictographs.* Duluth, Minn.: Birch Portage Press, 2000.

Gates, Barbara T. *Victorian and Edwardian Women Embrace the Living World.* Chicago: University of Chicago Press, 1998.

Gilman, Carolyn. *The Grand Portage Story.* St. Paul: Minnesota Historical Society Press, 1992.

Grant, Campbell. *The Rock Art of the North American Indians.* New York: Cambridge University Press, 1983.

Grant, W. L., ed. *Voyages of Samuel de Champlain, 1604–1618.* New York: C. Scribner's Sons, 1907.

The Great Lakes: An Environmental Atlas and Resource Book. 3d ed. Government of Canada and U.S. Environmental Protection Agency, 1995.

Great Lakes Bedrock Shores of Michigan. Michigan Natural Features Inventory, 1997.

Green, John C. *Geology on Display: Geology and Scenery of Minnesota's North Shore Parks.* St. Paul: Minnesota Department of Natural Resources, 1996.

Halsey, John R. *Miskwabik-Red Metal: The Roles Played by Michigan's Copper in Prehistoric North America.* Keweenaw County Historical Society, 1992.

Hansen, Arby, ed. *Cuy-una! A Chronicle of the Cuyuna Range.* Cuyuna Range Bicentennial Committee, 1976.

Harnsberger, John L. *Jay Cooke and Minnesota: The Formative Years of the Northern Pacific Railroad, 1868–1873.* New York: Arno Press, 1981.

Harp, Maureen Anna. *Indian Missions, Immigrant Migrations, and Regional Catholic Culture: Slovene Missionaries in the Upper Great Lakes, 1830–1892.* Ph.D. diss., University of Chicago, 1996.

Harris, James T., and Sumner W. Matteson. *Gulls and Terns as Indicators of Man's Impact upon Lake Superior.* Madison: University of Wisconsin Sea Grant College Program, 1975.

———. "Gulls and Terns Nesting at Duluth." *The Loon* 47, 2 (summer 1975).

Harris, Walter J. *The Chequamegon Country, 1659–1976.* Fayetteville, Ark.: Harris, 1976.

Heinselman, Miron. *The Boundary Waters Wilderness Ecosystem.* Minneapolis: University of Minnesota Press, 1996.

Hellander, Martha E. *The Wild Gardener: The Life and Selected Writings of Eloise Butler.* St. Cloud, Minn.: North Star Press, 1992.

Hertzel, Anthony X., and Robert B. Janssen. *County Nesting Records of Minnesota Birds.* Minneapolis: Minnesota Ornithologists' Union Occasional Paper No. 2, 1998.

Hill, Elaine A. *A Guide to Head-of-the-Lakes Wild Flowers of Northwestern*

Wisconsin and Northeastern Minnesota. Mountain View, Calif.: Moonlith Press, 1975.

Holbrook, Sabra. *The French Founders of North America and Their Heritage.* New York: Atheneum, 1976.

Holman, J. Alan. *Ancient Life in the Great Lakes Basin: Precambrian to Pleistocene.* Ann Arbor: University of Michigan Press, 1995.

Holmquist, June Drenning. *They Chose Minnesota: A Survey of the State's Ethnic Groups.* St. Paul: Minnesota Historical Society Press, 1981.

Holzhueter, John O. *Madeline Island and the Chequamegon Region.* Madison: State Historical Society of Wisconsin, 1986.

Humphrey, M. J., Adolph A. Toftey, and Willis H. Raff. *Faces and Places II: A Cook County Album, 1930–1960.* Grand Marais, Minn.: Cook County Historical Society, 1985.

Innis, Harold A. *The Fur Trade in Canada.* New Haven: Yale University Press, 1930.

Jerrard, Leigh P. *The Brule River of Wisconsin.* Chicago: Hall and Son, 1956.

Kellogg, Louise Phelps. "The French Regime in the Great Lakes Country." *Minnesota History* 12, 4 (December 1931): 347–58.

Kennedy, John H. *Jesuit and Savage in New France.* New Haven, Conn.: Yale University Press, 1950.

Kent, Edna, ed. *Black Gowns and Redskins: Adventures and Travels of the Early Jesuit Missionaries in North America.* London and New York: Longmans, Green, 1956.

Kramer, Jack. *Women of Flowers: A Tribute to Victorian Women Illustrators.* New York: Stewart Tabori and Chang, 1996.

Krupp, E. C. *Echoes of the Ancient Sky: The Astronomy of Lost Civilizations.* New York: Oxford University Press, 1994.

LaBerge, Gene L. *Geology of the Lake Superior Region.* Tucson, Ariz.: Geoscience Press, 1994.

LaBoule, Joseph Stephen. *Allouez and His Relations to LaSalle.* Madison: State Historical Society of Wisconsin, 1899.

Lake Superior Binational Program, Superior Work Group. *Lake Superior Lakewide Management Plan 2000.* April 2000.

Lamb, Kaye W. *The History of Canada: From Discovery to Present Day.* New York: American Heritage Press, 1971.

Larson, Agnes M. *History of the White Pine Industry in Minnesota.* Minneapolis: University of Minnesota Press, 1949.

Larson, Henrietta M. *Jay Cooke: Private Banker.* Cambridge: Harvard University Press, 1936.

Laut, Agnes C. *Pathfinders of the West.* New York: Macmillan Publ., 1923.

Ley, Willy. *Watchers of the Skies: An Informal History of Astronomy from Babylon to the Space Age.* New York: Viking Press, 1963.

Lomasney, Patrick J. "The Canadian Jesuits and the Fur Trade." *Mid-America* 15, 3 (January 1933).

Luecke, John C. *The Great Northern in Minnesota: The Foundations of an Empire.* St. Paul, Minn.: Grenadier Publications, 1997.

Lund, Duane R. *Our Historic Boundary Waters: From Lake Superior to Lake of the Woods.* Cambridge, Minn.: Adventure Publications, 1980.

Marshall, Albert M. *Brule Country.* St. Paul, Minn.: North Central Pub., 1954.

Martin, Ron, and Carl Gawboy. *Talking Rocks: Geology and 10,000 Years of Native American Tradition in the Lake Superior Region.* Duluth, Minn.: Pfeifer-Hamilton Publishers, 2000.

Mattson, Hans. *Den Nya Svenska Kolonien i Minnesota, Nord-Amerika: Goda Land för Emigranter, på de Billigaste Vilkor Vid Lake Superior Jernbanan.* 1872. Reprint, Stockholm: Rediviva, 1970.

———. *Reminiscences: The Story of an Emigrant.* St. Paul, Minn.: D. D. Merrill Co., 1892.

McCullough, David. *The American Adventure of Louis Agassiz.* New York: National Audubon Society, 1977.

McDonough, Peter. *Men Astutely Trained: A History of the Jesuits in the American Century.* New York: Maxwell Macmillan, 1992.

Medlin, Julie Jones. *Michigan Lichens.* Bloomfield Hills, Mich.: Cranbrook Institute of Science, Bulletin 60, 1996.

Miall, L. C. *The Early Naturalists: Their Lives and Work (1530–1789).* London: MacMillan and Co., 1912.

Minnesota Historical Records Survey Project. *The Cuyuna Range: A History of a Minnesota Iron and Mining District.* St. Paul, Minn.: The Project, 1940.

Minnesota State Board of Immigration. *Minnesota och dess Fördelar för Invandraren.* Chicago: Svenska Amerikanarens Boktryckeri, 1867.

Monroe, Jean, Ray Williamson, and Edgar Stewart. *They Dance in the Sky: Native American Star Myths.* Boston: Houghton Mifflin, 1987.

Moore, James T. *Indian and Jesuit: A Seventeenth-Century Encounter.* Chicago: Loyola University Press, 1982.

Morris, Bishop. *Champlain: The Life of Fortitude.* New York: A. A. Knopf, 1948.

Morrison, Samuel E. *Samuel de Champlain: Father of New France.* Boston: Little, Brown, and Co., 1972.

Mulholland, Susan C. "The Arrowhead Since the Glaciers: A Prehistory of Northeastern Minnesota." *Minnesota Archaeologist* 59 (2000).

Murray, Joan. *The Best of the Group of Seven.* Toronto: McClelland and Stewart, 1993.

Neill, Edward D. *The History of Minnesota: From the Earliest French Explorations to the Present Time.* Minneapolis: Minnesota Historical Society, 1883.

Newlands, Anne. *The Group of Seven and Tom Thomson: An Introduction.* Willowdale, Ontario: Firefly Books, 1995.

Newman, Peter C. *Company of Adventurers.* New York: Viking, 1985.

Nute, Grace Lee. *Caesars of the Wilderness: Médard Chouart, Sieur des Groseilliers, and Pierre Esprit Radisson, 1618–1710.* New York: D. Appleton-Century Co., 1943.

———. *Lake Superior.* 1944. Reprint, Minneapolis: University of Minnesota Press, 2000.

Oberholtzer, Ellis Paxson. *Jay Cooke: Financier of the Civil War.* Philadelphia: George W. Jacobs and Co., 1907.

Ogilvie, Marilyn, and Joy Harvey, eds. *The Biographical Dictionary of Women in Science.* New York: Routledge, 2000.

Ojakangas, Richard W., and Charles L. Matsch. *Minnesota's Geology.* Minneapolis: University of Minnesota Press, 1982.

Parkman, Francis. *The Jesuits in North America. France and England in North America, Part 2.* Boston: Little, Brown, and Co., 1867.

———. *Pioneers of France in the New World. France and England in North America, Part 1.* Boston: Little, Brown, and Co., 1865.

Peattie, Donald Culross. *Green Laurels: The Lives and Achievements of the Great Naturalists.* New York: Garden City Publishing Co., 1938.

Peters, Bernard C. *Lake Superior Place Names: From Bawating to the Montreal.* Marquette: Northern Michigan University Press, 1996.

Peters, Gordon R. "Tracking Minnesota's Ancient People." *Minnesota Conservation Volunteer* 44, 257 (July/August 1981).

Peterson, Harold F. "Early Minnesota Railroads and the Quest for Settlers." *Minnesota History* 13, 1 (March 1932): 25–44.

———. "Some Colonization Projects of the Northern Pacific Railroad." *Minnesota History* 10, 2 (June 1929): 127–44.

Phillips, Brian A. M., and Christopher L. Hill. *The Geology, Glacial and Shoreline History, and Archaeological Potential of the Minnesota North Shore of Lake Superior.* Archaeometry Laboratory, University of Minnesota-Duluth. St. Paul: Minnesota Department of Natural Resources, Division of Parks and Recreation, 1994.

Quimby, George Irving. *Indian Life in the Upper Great Lakes 11,000 B.C. to A.D. 1800.* 1960. Reprint, Berkeley: University of California Press, 1983.

Raff, Willis H. *Law and Order in the Wilderness.* Grand Marais, Minn.: Cook County Historical Society, 1982.

———. *Pioneers in the Wilderness: Minnesota's Cook County, Grand Marais, and the Gunflint Trail in the Nineteenth Century.* Grand Marais, Minn.: Cook County Historical Society, 1981.

Rafferty, Michael, and Robert Sprague. *Porcupine Mountains Companion: Inside Michigan's Largest State Park.* 3d ed. White Pine, Mich.: Nequaket Natural History Associates, 1996.

Ross, Frank E. "The Fur Trade of the Western Great Lakes Region." *Minnesota History* 19, 3 (September 1938): 271–307.

Ross, Hamilton Nelson. *La Pointe: Village Outpost.* St. Paul, Minn.: North Central Publishing Co., 1960.

Runblom, Harald, and Hans Norman, eds. *From Sweden to America: A History of the Migration. Uppsala Migration Research Project.* Minneapolis: University of Minnesota Press, 1976.

Ryan, J. C. *Early Loggers in Minnesota.* Vol. 1. Duluth, Minn.: Minnesota Timber Producers Association, 1975.

Ryder, John P. "Ring-Billed Gull." *The Birds of North America.* No. 33. Philadelphia: The Birds of North America, 1993.

Sagard, Gabriel. *The Long Journey to the Country of the Hurons.* 1632. Ed. George M. Wrong. Trans. by H. H. Langton. Toronto: The Champlain Society, 1939.

Schoolcraft, Henry Rowe. *The Indian Tribes of the United States: Their Antiquities, Customs, Religion, Arts, Language, Traditions, Oral Legends, and Myths.* Philadelphia: Lippincott, 1884.

Searle, R. Newell. *Saving Quetico-Superior: A Land Set Apart.* St. Paul: Minnesota Historical Society Press, 1977.

————. *State Parks of the North Shore.* Minnesota State Parks Heritage Series, no. 3. Minnesota Parks Foundation, 1979.

Sedgwick, Henry Dwight. *Samuel de Champlain.* Boston: Houghton, Mifflin, and Co., 1902.

Setterdahl, Lilly. *Minnesota Swedes: The Emigration from Trolle Ljungby to Goodhue County.* East Moline, Ill.: American Friends of the Emigrant Institute of Sweden, 1996.

Shea, John G. *Discovery and Exploration of the Mississippi Valley: With the Original Narratives of Marquette, Allouez, Membré, Hennepin, and Anastase Douay.* Albany, N.Y.: J. McDonough, 1903.

Sibley, David. *National Audubon Society: The Sibley Guide to Birds.* New York: Knopf, 2000.

Slade, Andrew, ed. *Guide to the Superior Hiking Trail: Linking People with Nature by Footpath along Lake Superior's North Shore.* Two Harbors, Minn.: Ridgeline Press, 1993.

Staal, Julius D. W. *Patterns in the Sky: Myths and Legends of the Stars.* Blacksburg, Va.: McDonald and Woodward Publishing Company, 1988.

Stensas, Mark. *Canoe Country Flora: Plants and Trees of the North Woods and Boundary Waters.* Duluth, Minn.: Pfeifer-Hamilton Publishers, 1996.

Stevens, Wayne E. "The Fur Trade in Minnesota during the British Regime." *Minnesota History Bulletin* 5, 1 (February 1923).

Strand, Algot E. *A History of the Swedish-Americans of Minnesota.* Chicago: Lewis Publishing, 1910.

Tester, John R. *Minnesota's Natural Heritage: An Ecological Perspective.* Minneapolis: University of Minnesota Press, 1995.

Thwaites, Reuben Gold. *The Jesuit Relations and Allied Documents: Travels and Explorations of the Jesuit Missionaries in New France, 1610–1791.* Cleveland, Ohio: Burrows Bros., Co., 1896–1901.

Titman, Rodger D. "Red-Breasted Merganser." *The Birds of North America.* No. 443. Philadelphia: The Birds of North America, 1999.

U.S. Fish and Wildlife Service. *Waterfowl Population Status, 2001.* Washington, D.C.: U.S. Department of the Interior, 2001.

Upham, Warren. *Minnesota in Three Centuries: Descriptions and Explorations.* Vol. 1. New York: Publishing Society of Minnesota, 1908.

————. *Minnesota Place Names: A Geographical Encyclopedia.* 3d ed. St. Paul: Minnesota Historical Society Press, 2001.

Vecsey, Christopher. *Traditional Ojibwa Religion and Its Historical Changes.* Philadelphia: American Philosophical Society, 1990.

Veenendaal, A. J. *The Saint Paul & Pacific Railroad: An Empire in the Making, 1862–1879.* Dekalb: Northern Illinois University Press, 1999.

Verwyst, Chrysostom. *Missionary Labors of Fathers Marquette, Menard, and Allouez in the Lake Superior Region.* Milwaukee and Chicago: Hoffmann Brothers, 1886.

Vestal, Stanley. *King of the Fur Traders: The Deeds and Deviltry of Pierre Esprit Radisson.* Boston: Houghton Mifflin Co., 1940.

Wade, Mason. *The French Canadians, 1760–1967.* Vol. 1. Toronto: Macmillan Co. of Canada, 1968.

Waters, Thomas F. *The Streams and Rivers of Minnesota.* Minneapolis: University of Minnesota Press, 1977.

————. *The Superior North Shore: A Natural History of Lake Superior's Northern Lands and Waters.* Minneapolis: University of Minnesota Press, 1987.

Whelan, Robert J. *The Ecology of Fire.* Cambridge: Cambridge University Press, 1995.

Williamson, Ray A. *Living the Sky: The Cosmos of the American Indian.* Norman: University of Oklahoma Press, 1984.

Williamson, Ray A., and Claire R. Farrer. *Earth and Sky: Visions of the Cosmos in Native American Folklore.* Albuquerque: University of New Mexico Press, 1992.

Wirth, Fremont P. *The Discovery and Exploitation of the Minnesota Iron Lands.* Cedar Rapids, Iowa: Torch Press, 1937.

Wolter, Scott F. *The Lake Superior Agate.* 3d ed. Edina, Minn.: Burgess Pub., 1996.

Woodbridge, Dwight E., and John S. Pardee, eds. *History of Duluth and St. Louis County: Past and Present.* Vol. 2. Chicago: C. F. Cooper and Co., 1910.

Yost, Edna. *American Women of Science.* Philadelphia: Lippincott, 1955.

ERIKA ALIN is a teacher, writer, and photographer who lives in Saint Paul, Minnesota. Her nature writing has appeared in *Natural Superior* and other magazines, and her photography of Lake Superior has been included in numerous exhibits and publications. She teaches at Hamline University.